Work in Progress:
Migration, Integration and the European Labour Market

Work in Progress: Migration, Integration and the European Labour Market

Mikel Azurmendi
David Coleman
Tamar Jacoby
Robert Rowthorn
Juan José Toribio

Editor: Helen Disney

Civitas: Institute for the Study of Civil Society
London

First published May 2003

The Mezzanine, Elizabeth House
39 York Road, London SE1 7NQ
email: books@civitas.org.uk

ISBN 1-903 386-28 4

Typeset by Civitas
in New Century Schoolbook

Printed in Great Britain by
Hartington Fine Arts
Lancing, Sussex

Contents

Acknowledgement

Work in Progress is based on a seminar organised by the Stockholm Network and the Circulo de Empresarios (Madrid's Business Round Table) in Summer 2002. The Stockholm Network and Civitas would like to thank the Circulo for all their help in making the seminar and the book possible.

The Stockholm Network is a dedicated network of European market-oriented think tanks based at Civitas in London. Its members include Timbro in Stockholm, the Centre for the New Europe in Brussels and the Edmund Burke Foundation in The Hague.

Authors

Mikel Azurmendi chairs Spain's Forum for the Social Integration of Immigrants, which was convened in 2000. He was born in the Basque country. Bilingual in Spanish and Basque, he was forced into exile for his nationalist stance in the late Sixties. A Professor at the Sorbonne during his exile, he returned to Spain to teach as a Professor of Anthropology at the University of the Basque Country. He has written several books in Basque and has been called 'an anthropologist without a tribe' because of his opposition to the tribal nature of mainstream Basque nationalism, particularly in its most violent forms. He was the first spokesman of the 'Foro de Ermua', and a founding member of 'Basta Ya' (That's Enough), two organisations that have led support for the victims of terrorism and the civilian rebellion against terror.

David Coleman is Reader in Demography at Oxford University. He was formerly Lecturer in Physical Anthropology at University College London. Between 1985 and 1987 he worked for the British government as a Special Adviser to the Home Secretary and then to the Ministers of Housing and the Environment. He has worked as a consultant for the Home Office, the UN and private business. He was joint editor of the *European Journal of Population* (Paris) from 1992 to 2000 and in 1997 was elected to the Council of the International Union for the Scientific Study of Population. His research interests include the comparative demographic trends of the industrial world, particularly the reasons for the persistence of substantial international differences in birth and death rates and in family structure. He is also interested in immigration trends and the demography of ethnic minorities and has published extensively on these topics.

Helen Disney divides her time between running the Stockholm Network, Europe's only dedicated network for market-oriented think-tanks, based at Civitas in London, and writing articles for a variety of publications including *The Times* of London, the *Daily Express* and *Sunday Express*, *Public Finance*, *Public Service Magazine*, and the Centre for the New Europe's health weblog (www.cnehealth.org). She previously worked as a leader writer for *The Times* and for four years at the Social Market Foundation, an independent pro-market think-tank in Westminster, where she was Deputy Director and Editor of *The Review*, a quarterly journal.

Tamar Jacoby is senior fellow at the Manhattan Institute where she writes extensively on race, ethnicity and other subjects. Her 1998 book, *Someone Else's House: America's Unfinished Struggle for Integration*, tells the story of race relations in New York, Detroit and Atlanta. Her articles and book reviews have been published in a host of periodicals, including the *New York Times*, the *Wall Street Journal*, the *Washington Post*, the *Los Angeles Times*, the *New Republic*, *National Review*, the *Weekly Standard*, *Commentary*, the *New York Review of Books*, the *Washington Monthly*, *Dissent*, *Foreign Affairs*, *City Journal* and the *Times Literary Supplement*. Before joining the Manhattan Institute, she was a senior writer and justice editor for *Newsweek*, deputy editor of the *New York Times* op-ed page and assistant to the editor of the *New York Review of Books*.

Robert Rowthorn is professor of Economics at Cambridge University and Fellow of King's College, Cambridge. He has written extensively on inflation, employment and globalisation. He has also frequently worked as a consultant on these topics for the ILO, the IMF and UNCTAD.

Juan José Toribio is head of the IESE, a distinguished Spanish post-graduate business school, and writes regularly for *Expansion* (www.expansion.com). He holds a Doctorate in Economics from Chicago University. From 1970 to 1975 he was an Economist at the Bank of Spain and then Director General for Financial Policy at the Ministry of Economy from 1977-1979. He has been director of several financial institutions, including an Executive Directorship at the IMF. He is also a board member of the investment bank Invercaixa and of Xfera (a telecoms firm) and has been Chairman of AIAF (an organised market for fixed-income instruments) and Vice-Chairman of MEFF (the Spanish Derivatives Market).

Introduction

Helen Disney

Globalisation has created a host of benefits, not least the freer movement of goods and services needed to bring greater economic prosperity to the world. But along with the freer movement of goods and services comes a greater demand for other types of freedom, including a desire to share in the benefits of economic prosperity by migrating to countries where jobs and other benefits are more plentiful.

Since the relaxation of its national borders, migration into and between the countries of the European Union has become far more common and has begun to raise an urgent series of policy dilemmas. How can immigrants be better integrated into society? Is the labour market flexible enough to accommodate all those who want to come here to work? What will be the impact of greater diversity on our national identity? Should we be limiting the influx of newcomers into our countries and, if so, how can we do this and how strict do we need to be?

This collection of essays shows that the process of dealing with increasing migration into Europe and its impact on our welfare states and labour markets is still very much a work in progress. Policy experts are divided on whether we need more immigrants to deal with Europe's ageing population or whether this is merely an economic myth. They are also divided on how severe the social impact of absorbing so many new cultures will be.

Mikel Azurmendi, President of the Spanish Forum for the Social Integration of Immigrants, describes his personal experience of the shortcomings of multiculturalism, especially in the Basque Country and in the Spanish outpost of Melilla in Africa. He argues that multiculturalism does more harm than good by leading to the creation of divided communities or 'monocultures' which do not integrate with one another. The solution, he says, is better education and more practical help for immigrants so that they are able to regain their dignity and build a stable home life. Only then does he think that integration stands any chance of success.

David Coleman, Reader in Demography at Oxford University, also argues against mass immigration as a means of solving the problems of Europe's ageing population. According to his calculations, the numbers needed in order to maintain the current support ratio (i.e. the number of people of working age needed to support elderly non-workers) would make life in Britain unrecognisable and untenable.

The consequences of migration are not just economic but political and cultural and so, he concludes, our response to this policy question has profound implications for the British way of life. Fellow academic Bob Rowthorn of Cambridge University concurs that Fortress Europe is perhaps wrongly coined as a negative term.

Juan José Toribio, Director of the IESE, a respected Spanish post-graduate business school, proposes a more open, flexible, EU-wide immigration policy. He argues that Spain's appalling employment record stems far more from its entrenched labour market inflexibility and the size of its welfare state than from any threat theoretically posed by immigration.

Giving a view from across the pond, Tamar Jacoby, Senior Fellow at the Manhattan Institute, an American market-oriented think-tank, argues that almost all the good things about the United States are the result of immigration. She also wonders whether it is time for European nations to face up to the challenges of assimilation and allow for more open channels for legal immigration rather than burying their heads in the sand and trying to maintain a Fortress Europe.

By publishing these essays, along with a series of others on the immigration question, Civitas and the Stockholm Network hope to stimulate an honest debate about the host of questions raised by the freer movement of human capital that globalisation is bringing about. If we wish to glory in the benefits that immigration may bring we must also accept that such a radical change in our social structure has the potential to cause problems. Unless we are sensible about dealing with them now, both Europe and those many people who wish to make a new life here will only be the poorer.

Is multi-culturalism helping or hindering integration in Spain?

Mikel Azurmendi

I cannot give a definitive reply to this question because, effectively, our experience is still inadequate. Spain has spread people all over the world and there are still hundreds of thousands of Spaniards in Europe working as economic migrants or living as political immigrants. But immigration into Spain is still a relatively new experience, which hardly allows us to preach on the question.

However, in Europe we all have our own experiences of democracy, of cultural pluralism and of tolerance. Some more than others have traditions of historical integration. Yet Spain cannot claim to have had a strong tradition of integration. For example, we were often intolerant towards those who practised another religion, at least until the foundation of the nation state from the fourteenth to the nineteenth century.

Recently in Spain we have experienced some controversy over the issue of integrating immigrants. When I went to the Senate to meet the group studying the integration of immigrants to explain how the integration of immigrants was happening as I saw it personally, I established that some of them saw Spain's model for the social integration of immigrants as being similar to Toledo from the tenth to the thirteenth or fourteenth century. This was a society in which three sectors of people lived side by side but without any kind of contact, except that of being neighbours. They were divided into three communities: Jewish, Islamic or Muslim, and Christian.

I was horrified by this dialogue. Why would we go about designing a future for Spain in which immigrants would make their own communities and Spaniards our own separate communities? Of course, I explained that the right thing to do was to socially integrate them into our culture. Then I said: 'Look here, multi-culturalism, which is not integration, but rather a juxtaposition, a segmentation into societies, into micro-societies, into mono-cultures, cannot lead to any kind of democratic future. Moreover, this is a great illness.' I called it gangrene and I continue to think of it as such. So you can see where the limits of the discussion lie. It hasn't got any further than this in Spain.

On the plus side, however, there is now a capacity to respond to the challenges we face. Our society is 25 years old. It is a quarter of a century since we voted for the first time, after a very long time indeed. Before that, we had 50 years when not only did we not vote but we also had great repression and a fundamental exclusion of that which was different. There was exclusion from within of those who typically became known as the mason, the communist, the red or the separatist. These were the people who did not have a future in Spain. But then, after Franco died, the inclusion of Spaniards into one society became possible, precisely because we all forsook something in order to accept a common future, of tolerating each other, respecting the same laws and being equal before the laws but with guarantees that each human being is different from the next.

Our democratic tradition is short. But we have other traditions, for example, Madrid. Madrid is a mix of generations and generations of different Spaniards, much more so than any other European capital. The problem that we solved in Spain 25 years ago, and which we have strengthened, is the problem of including everyone from a legal-political point of view. But we have yet to solve the problem of cultural immigration.

The main key to integration was the law and the political agreement to uphold the law. We are all equal, and for people to have autonomy, groups of people who have common complaints must have political representation. They should be politically accepting of the general state of things, of the democratic state of Spain.

We have solved some of the problems of Catalonia, the Basque Country and Galicia, for example, by finding a political solution, so that today in Spain the autonomy of the citizen is always guaranteed. This is fundamental because, as Jürgen Habermas says in his great book *The Inclusion of the Other*, we need to counterbalance what are called 'minorities'. We only talk about 'minorities' in terms of democratic representation and nothing more. We don't describe taxi drivers or baseball players or basketball players as a minority, even though they are of course minorities. Neither do we describe those who use public transport as the majority. For example there is a majority who catch the metro over those who use taxis in Madrid, but it never occurs to anyone to refer to those using taxis as the minority. This is a provocative example because the multi-culturalists automatically treat immigrants as though they were minorities, as though they were users of services for which they were going to be relegated to the status of minority, and would not *a priori* be treated like the majority.

Yet Spain is unique in Europe for the deterioration of our social fabric. What democracy has partially solved, could probably have been better resolved. In other words, we still haven't found the solution to the Basque problem. Why? Precisely because, thanks to democracy, we have achieved the separation of society into ethnic groups—something that the Basques themselves did not do even under the totalitarian régime of Franco.

The Basque Country is a multi-cultural and multi-culturalist society. They not only see Spain as different but also as the enemy. They have an ancient dispute with Spain, which cannot be solved except by separation from Spain. Put in even stronger terms, you would have to scare, terrorise or kill all those Basques who defend their choice to be Spanish citizens.

In the Basque Country multi-culturalism exists. There is the creation of a régime that favours certain people over others. Under the Pact of Estella-Lizarra, ETA together with the PNV and the communists or the United Left (IU) agreed to the political and ideological exclusion of all those who are not 'nationalists' i.e. those who see themselves represented by the major Spanish parties, who at the moment would be 95 per cent the Partido Popular (PP) and the Partido Socialista Obrero Español (PSOE). This is political exclusion.

Cultural exclusion is also a daily occurrence in the Basque education system via their school curriculum, their primary schools, various forms of indoctrination and the forging of a national spirit—something that the Falangistas (the former Spanish Fascist Party) and the Francoists tried to create in a similar way—through television and radio and the cultural exclusion of all that is Spanish. They have even erased the word Spain, which doesn't exist in the Basque Country. Instead of saying Spain, they all say 'the Spanish State', because they perceive Spain in the way it was under Franco, as a totalitarian state. This multi-cultural experience goes hand in hand with ethnic cleansing. This is not at an early stage but fairly advanced.

To integrate immigrants into Spain it would be enough to do the opposite of what has been done in the Basque Country. There, 75 per cent of people don't understand Basque. Nevertheless, they prohibit the use or teaching of Spanish in their schools. They have tried to make it so that Castilian does not exist in schools—and now it practically doesn't exist. Briefly, many of us here in Spain understand the social integration of immigrants as a symmetrical process, very similar to that of the disintegration of the social and civil fabric of the Basque Country but in reverse.

Another example of social disintegration is the example of Melilla, which I have visited on various occasions to examine the issue of multi-culturalism. Melilla, is not a creation of democracy, rather the opposite. It was created by the Francoist régime, and above all, by previous régimes. In Melilla, which is part of Spain and therefore part of Europe in Africa, there are two juxtaposed, segregated societies, where pedestrians pass by each other and live in the same city but have nothing in common. Those from Melilla who are of Moroccan origin are called 'Muslims' and vice versa they call us ‘Christians’. They call me a Christian even though I’m not one. Yet in Melilla I am treated as a Christian. They have thus managed to create communities in the name of two cultures (or in reality four, because there are also 200 Hindus and 1,000 Jews). They say it is a country of four cultures. In fact, it is a multi-cultural country in which two communities practically don’t even meet. The majority of the community is, at present, poor and excluded. They are excluded from the benefits of the welfare state, not just theoretically but practically.

In the last 25 years in Melilla there has been a great effort to tackle the segregation of different ethnicities. The Spanish Government as well as the European Union are injecting a large quantity of human and economic resources into the area so that schools and social services will offer more egalitarian treatment. However, it is still very difficult to achieve this when the two communities have a tradition of not meeting each other, of not mixing together. So, in Spain we already have two multi-cultural societies or monocultures that do not interrelate with each other or hardly ever relate to each other—the Basque Country and Melilla.

So what is the derivation of this notion of multi-culturalism? The word ‘multi-cultural’ does not come from Spain but from the large democratic country of Canada. In Canada, at the end of the 1960s and at the beginning of the 1970s, Pierre Trudeau decided to solve the problem of Anglophonic hegemony by a cultural readjustment so that the two cultures—the Anglophile and the Francophile—were considered more or less equal. The word multi-cultural was mentioned, keeping in mind the Indian communities who had been linguistically excluded. You perhaps know the constitution, the law of the rights and liberties of 1982? It seems to me that it is here that it is publicly announced that Canada is bilingual, and that in Canada there exist two communities, and where they then speak marginally and indirectly of other communities. These other communities waste money. They are granted constitutional rights, acquire more privileges, and in some way use these to milk the state. The state treats them hardly any better than it did before, but multi-culturalism still exists in Canada. The Secretary of State for Canada has edited some pages where he explains what multi-culturalism is, and where one can see the disadvantaged communities. Of course, if the multi-cultural outlook is the result of these pages, which give data about exclusion, unemployment, crime figures and details of those who commit them, then what is happening in Canada with immigrants is not encouraging. Nevertheless, the tradition in Canada is to solve a political problem in a cultural way, in the name of multi-culturalism. They have avoided what we have not managed to avoid. Why is there no ETA in Canada? Probably because there was no Franco in Canada.

Canadians talk much about multi-culturalism. There are already books which criticise it ruthlessly. Every country has to find its own path. I think that talking about models is not helpful. Academics in Spain, for example, and also in France, have dedicated a great deal of time to talking about models, about the 'assimilationist' model in France or the American 'melting-pot', the more homogenous British model, the multi-cultural model of the Netherlands or Sweden, Australia and Canada. I think that models can serve to explain the past, and to write about the past. But, for the future, what must be studied in more depth are the resources of each country and, from their own contexts of pluralism and tolerance, how they plan to deal with the integration of these immigrants. Without doubt, the majority of them want to stay among us. I don't have a single model, but I defend a model based on the real situation in Spain at this moment. The great defect that we have is the lack of civic education. In schools the Spanish government favours the teaching of religion over the teaching of ethics, tolerance, and cultural pluralism. Yet there is still time, government officials could talk to many people like me, and travel to the countries where this happens, for example, in the Netherlands, and more recently in Germany where the schools in Bratenburg have decided to teach Islam, and are starting teach languages such as Arabic and Turkish.

Bearing in mind the present state of things in Spain, it would be sensible to make immigrants accept the main characteristics of our own culture. There is already an assimilated democratic culture even though there are some undemocratic sectors of Spanish society. The backbone of civil society is supported by juridicial and political concepts, such as equality, law and law making.

What is the democratic state? It is the search for truth, which will not come from reading the Bible or the Koran, and the search for truth through discussion. This is something that many Basques have not yet learnt how to do. This backbone is essential for everyone to belong to this country. It is essential not only for Muslims but also for Ecuadorians, Dominicans, Colombians and Lithuanians. Therefore, you cannot live in Spain without studying Spanish, Catalan or Basque. Even so it is very difficult to be Catalan only speaking Catalan, or only speaking Basque.* Studying Spanish is another way to integrate oneself.

The requirement to know our language, as well as to know, understand and accept the main aspects of civil society and its place within the social order, the search for civic values, such as the values of public life, the search for truth, participation in debate, decency, not harming others with our actions: all these together are known as justice, tolerance and pluralism. We should create public and private schools based upon these values, so that immigrants and their children can participate like the rest of us.

Other key factors such as styles and ways of life, why people live under the influence of certain ethical, religious or aesthetic motivations, food, their way of clothing, and so on, should be left to the free will of each individual. Everyone is free to choose his way of dressing, he is free to go to a Catholic church or Protestant church or synagogue. These decisions are of no concern to us; these are private decisions made by each individual.

---

* Azurmendi is trying to say here that because in the Basque Country less than 25 per cent of the population speak Basque, learning Basque will not help immigrants to integrate in that region of Spain.

To achieve this integration we must somehow break down all these ethnic barriers, which each community tries to fortify with ideas, beliefs and ideologies, but also with lies, as in the Basque Country. We should fight this trend.

I think school is the key. There are also unsolved problems such as the home being a fundamentally important place for the formation of the individual. Spain has a major problem with this because we have not made a serious enough effort to help our children set up their own home. Spain is probably the European country in which children leave their homes latest. My own son, who is 30, still lives at home with me and for the last two years his girlfriend has been living with us too.

This problem is even greater with immigrants. Without a right to housing, immigrants live crowded together with 15 or 20 people in small flats. This is a depressing symptom of how far we have to go. For without individual dignity there will be no integration.

Demographic, economic and social consequences of UK migration

David Coleman

Introduction

The migration tradition in Britain, as in many but not all European countries, is one of emigration, not immigration. Britain only became a net importer of people about 20 years ago. There was always some inflow of immigrants, of course, but until the Second World War only occasionally in numbers large enough to make a political or demographic impact.

In particular, Britain did not generally institute 'guest worker' polices on the lines of German, Austrian or Swiss policy. The only exception was the recruitment of 'European voluntary workers', many from displaced persons' camps, in the late 1940s to help with post-war reconstruction.[1] Many of those workers returned home, others assimilated. The whole experience was mostly trouble-free and today is almost entirely forgotten.

On the other hand, citizens of the Irish Republic and of all Commonwealth countries enjoyed free movement into the UK even after those countries became independent. Entry of Commonwealth citizens was not brought under the same rules as that of other foreign citizens until 1971. A small number of workers from the New (i.e non-European) Commonwealth were recruited for transport and service jobs. Most arrived on a more opportunistic basis or as spouses, dependants, students. The latter categories continue to arrive in large numbers. The work permit scheme has operated to recruit workers from all over the world since 1920, varying with the demands of the economy but usually in modest numbers until very recently (for a brief history up to 1990 see Coleman and Salt, Ch.11,12).[2] From the 1980s asylum claiming has grown from tiny numbers to an inflow of about 100,000 per year, making Britain the preferred asylum destination in Europe, contrary to all the intentions of successive governments.

Until 1997, the theory of British immigration policy was very clear. It was 'to keep to an irreducible minimum the number of people coming to Britain for permanent settlement with the exception of the need to satisfy the demands of the labour force, to fulfil obligations to dependants, and to international treaties on asylum'.[3]

This was generally interpreted as meaning low levels of immigration or no net immigration at all. For many years that expectation was partially satisfied. Net migration overall (all citizenships together, including British) was negative until the 1980s. However, net immigration from the New Commonwealth of non-European countries never fell below about 30,000 per year, counterbalanced by an even greater outflow of British citizens.

However, although the policy to minimize immigration did not change, it was clearly failing even before the Conservatives left office. Net immigration became positive around 1982 and rose steadily to reach 92,000 persons per year in 1997, the last year of Conservative government. All components of immigration increased. (Table 1, p. 11, Figure 1, p. 12). The Conservatives' asylum legislation of 1993 and 1996 conspicuously failed to stop the increase of asylum claiming. Official statements always played down the growth in numbers. The Commission for Racial Equality and various immigrant pressure groups tended to insist that the numbers were minimal, that drawing attention to them was racist, or in recent years when the huge inflow had become impossible to disguise, that we needed the immigrants anyway.

The actual figures for known immigration for 2000 given by the Office for National Statistics in 2002 showed a net inflow of 183,000 persons.[4] This did not include the dependants of asylum claimants, which are known to the Home Office but which are not given to the ONS for its calculations.[5] The addition of that figure, about 20,000 in recent years, would take the net inflow to over 200,000 for the year

2000. The unofficial migration monitoring organisation MigrationWatchUK,[6] to which this author acts as an honorary adviser, recently presented estimates of a total of 60,000 illegal immigrants and overstayers each year, not included in the total above. Although inevitably precarious and requiring arbitrary assumptions, these figures are modest compared most other estimates (no official estimate has been published). Taken together, net migration into the UK in 2000 would have been over 200,000 and net migration of foreign citizens over a quarter of a million.

Table 1
Some basic statistics on UK migration

	International Passenger Survey	**Home Office data**		
	net inflow (corrected)	spouses	work permit	asylum (inc. dependants)
1977	-46,100	24,474	12,381	
1987	+30,100	22,030	19,780	5,863
1997	+92,000	31,660	43,700	41,500
2000	+183,400	46,670	91,800	91,200

The data below all come from the corrected IPS estimates

		Citizenship		of which:
	Corrected net migration	British	Non-British	NC*
1977	-46,100	-70,700	24,500	10,700
1987	+30,100	-31,600	61,800	31,000
1997	+92,000	-34,300	128,600	45,800
2000	+183,400	-46,600	230,000	78,400

*NC: New Commonwealth

Note: The International Passenger Survey data, which include asylum claimants and visitor switchers, are used for demographic purposes. The Home Office data apply to foreign citizens only who are admitted under specific categories in the Immigration Rules. They are not generally compatible with the IPS data but give some idea of the components of flows.

Sources: Home Office, *Control of Immigration: Statistics United Kingdom 2000*, Cm 5315, London: The Stationery Office, 2001; ONS International Migration Statistics Series MN; Shaw, C., *Population Trends 91*, 1998; Home Office Statistical Bulletin 24/98; Home Office RDS, no. 67.

Figure 1
Net Immigration (2 definitions) and asylum 1981-2002

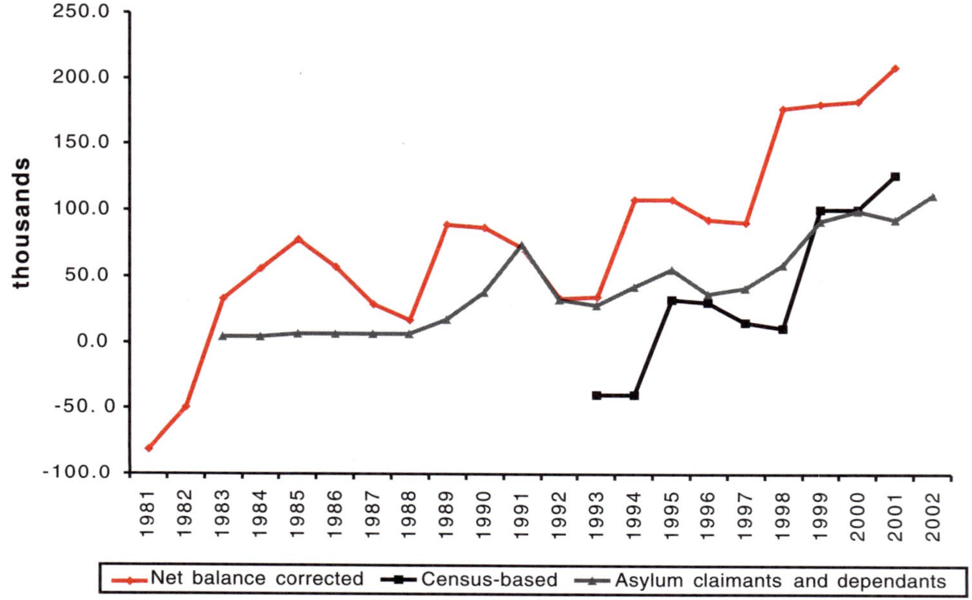

Demographic, economic and social consequences of migration to the UK

However, very recently the Office for National Statistics (ONS) has revised radically, and downwards, the estimates of net immigration to the UK. The results of the 2001 census apparently showed that the real UK population was 58.8 million, not the 60 million expected from the intercensal estimates. The huge expenditure and careful statistical planning of this census has persuaded the ONS that its results, though unexpected, must be infallible despite the very large number of imputations required to reach the final figure. Accordingly the most vulnerable element of the intercensal estimates, the international migration figures, have necessarily been 'blamed' for the the over-estimated population, as the easiest available culprit. Although no direct evidence has been adduced, the ONS has decided that the emigration of UK citizens has been cumulatively underestimated by about 800,000 persons over the last decade. Accordingly it has added 76,000 each year to the net emigration figures, thus reducing net immigration by 76,000 per year.[7]

These arbitrary Procrustean amputations, the effect of which is shown in Figure 1, are without precedent in international demographic statistics. Some critics do not accept either the infallibility of the census figures or the bludgeoning of the migration data to make them fit the census. Acceptance of the census figures requires the acceptance of the most bizarre sex-age structure of any national population in Europe, denies the evident effects of cumulative immigration in many areas, and has created a population of 800,000 missing UK males aged 20-50 who have allegedly failed to return from trips to places such as Australia, even though the excellent and computerized Australian statistics show no such result. Migration data for 2001 have not been released on the previous basis of calculation. However, as the census-based net figure has increased by 26,000 over that for the year 2000, it may be inferred that the 2001 net overall inflow on the former basis has now reached 209,000. ONS suspicions do not seem to have rested on the migration of non-UK citizens, so it may additionally be inferred that net immigration of foreign citizens in 2001 was 256,000 although no detailed break-downs were published at the time of going to press. The total of asylum claimants including accompanying dependants in 2002 has risen to 110,700 from the 2001 figure of 92,000. So further increases in overall migration estimates for 2002 may be expected.

The incoming Labour Government has had a rather uneven view about immigration. Previous Labour governments (1964-1970, 1974-1979) had not substantially challenged the immigration control policy established by the Conservative legislation in 1962 and 1971, although the Labour Party opposed the legislation when in opposition. Indeed, the Labour government strengthened it with new measures in 1965 and 1968. The initial statements by the incoming Labour government in 1997[8] did not seem radically different from those of its predecessor, although it did fulfil its promise to its ethnic minority supporters in acting quickly to facilitate more immigration for purposes of marriage and visits. The previous, central policy statement about 'minimising settlement' is now absent but the preamble to the first Labour policy statement still noted that: 'Every country must exercise firm control over immigration and Britain is no exception.'

Since 1998, however, the New Labour government has made a break from the previous consensus. Instead, it has urged a re-consideration of migration, suggesting that it should be regarded as an asset rather than a problem.[9] Official sources have extolled migration for its supposed economic, cultural, social and other benefits. In the 'respectable' media, enthusiasm for migration is now the norm. The editorial line in the *Guardian*, the *Independent*, the *Financial Times* and *The Economist* and even the right-wing weekly *Spectator* is that more migration is not only essential for our continued economic health but might be help to rescue us from our own reproductive indolence by sustaining our ageing population through 'replacement migration', satisfying demand for labour and diversifying our culture.

Even the middle-brow tabloid *Daily Express*, formerly anti-immigration, has sometimes joined the crowd. Only the *Daily Telegraph* (broadsheet) and the *Daily Mail* (tabloid) show concern about numbers. The release of immigration estimates by MigrationWatch UK in August 2002, mostly based on official numbers, was greeted with a venomous editorial in the *Independent* and by personal attacks on the report's authors in that and other 'liberal' papers. The front page of *The Economist* of 31 March 2001 exemplifies the position taken by those who claim the moral high ground. 'Let the huddled masses in', it proclaims, aping, as the British do with so many things, American slogans and American ideology in an inappropriate setting.

This enthusiasm is not entirely unqualified, however, as the new government, no doubt aware of popular opposition to migration, is careful to state that migration cannot be uncontrolled. However, it has never stated in any of the numerous speeches or papers on the subject what the limits might be, or what the effects on the population size, density and ethnic composition of the population will be as a result of its new policies. This ambiguity is apparent in the extracts given below. These involve various quotations from the 2001 White Paper (which set out various policy aims) and speeches by the former Immigration Minister, Barbara Roche.[10]

Ideas behind the Government's new migration policy

(i) Extracts from *Secure Border, Safe Haven: Integration with diversity in modern Britain*[11]

- Migration is inevitable and brings significant benefits.
- Integration with diversity is the aim.
- It is nonsense to talk of 'invasion' through the Channel Tunnel.
- It is mistaken to think of immigration to the UK as being an easy option.
- UK must uphold basic human rights.

- Those coming into our country have duties.
- A modern, flexible coherent immigration policy means welcoming those with a contribution to make, offering refuge, and engaging those who seek citizenship.
- Migration brings huge benefits: increased skills, enhanced levels of economic activity, cultural diversity, global links, but also can raise tensions.

Quotes from the debate about UK immigration policy, 2000-2002

Barbara Roche, Immigration Minister

- Britain has always been a nation of immigrants.
- The UK needs a policy that meets modern needs.
- Migration could help ease economic impact of (population ageing).
- Migration can play a positive role in the economy.
- Migrants ...are more resourceful, entrepreneurial and ambitious than the norm.
- The contribution migrants have made to the country is clear.
- There is no question about the continuing need for immigration control.

The statement quoted above that Britain has 'always been a nation of immigrants', now an official government mantra widely repeated in the media, by the Commission for Racial Equality and others, is demonstrably false on historical and demographic grounds. It reflects an unfortunate tendency of the present government either to be ignorant of history or to re-write it in its own interest with a more suitable spin. There has, of course, always been some movement into and out of Britain. But most episodes of immigration since the Dark Ages appear to have had limited demographic and genetic impact. Since the sixteenth century, episodes of immigration have been overshadowed demographically by emigration overseas.

Any ambiguity between the statement that 'there is no question about the continuing need for immigration control' and the other comments preparing the ground for more immigration has now in practice been resolved firmly in favour of immigration, which is now at by far the highest level ever recorded in British history even at the new, truncated ONS estimates. However, while government statements make no mention of limits on 'regular' migration, official rhetoric is firmly against uncontrolled asylum-claiming and illegal immigration while still emphasising a commitment to asylum. The previous and present Home Secretaries, Jack Straw and David Blunkett, and the current Prime Minister Tony Blair, have talked tough on illegal immigration and asylum, but so far their actions have been ineffectual in stemming the inflow.

Demographic consequences of immigration to date

What has the actual result been in terms of numbers? Up to about 1982, net migration was negative: as in previous centuries, the United Kingdom lost population through the process of migration. Since the early 1980s there has been a more or less clear upward trend until, for the last three years, net migration to Britain has been about 180,000 persons per year on the previous, pre-census definition. This annual total is equivalent to the size of a London borough such as Islington, Camden or Barking or a medium-sized city such as Oxford (140,000 people). In relation to population size (180,000 compared to 60 million: 0.3 per cent of population per year), this net inflow, which includes asylum claimants, is about the same as the gross annual legal inflow to the United States (800,000 addition to 284 million: also 0.3 per cent of population per year). As outflow from the US is usually reckoned to be about one-third of the gross inflow (it is not measured) total known net immigration to the UK for the three years up to 2000 was actually greater, relative to population size, than legal net immigration to the United States.

The UK data given above relate to immigration as defined by the United Nations, which needs to be clarified. The UN definition of an international migrant, employed by the UK International Passenger Survey, is a person who has lived abroad for at least 12 months, who has entered another country with the intention of staying there for at least 12 months. The inflow to the UK is a mixed flow of dependants, of new spouses through arranged marriage, of students, of workers and their dependants, and asylum claimants. There are no official data on illegal immigrants. Asylum claimants comprise an increasing proportion of this migration flow to the UK as to some other countries; about half the total in the year 2000. That flow comprised, in the year 2000, a net addition to the population of 230,000 foreign population and a net loss of about 45,000 British citizens. The 183,000 is a balance between an even bigger inflow of foreign population and a net outflow of British citizens. Estimates of the inflow of foreign citizens are not much disturbed by the new ONS revisions. However, as noted above, the ONS 2001 census data now claims that net outflow of UK citizens is 76,000 a year higher than supposed—which would take total UK citizen outflow to 121,000 per year.

The effect on the UK population depends somewhat on how it is measured. The most striking consequence of post-war immigration has been on the ethnic composition of the population. The population of non-white 'ethnic minority' origin in the UK as officially defined, mostly from the non-European countries of the New Commonwealth, comprised about 4.2 million persons in the year 2000. That population numbered perhaps 50,000 people in 1950. Over 50 years, non-European immigration and subsequent fertility has added an additional four million people to the British population, which today is 60 million and would otherwise have been 56 million (on pre-2001 census base).

The ethnic minority population of 4.6 million in 2001 (7.9 per cent) includes both those born abroad (immigrants) and their children and later descendants born in the UK, but excludes those foreigners (mostly Europeans or citizens of the US and the Old Commonwealth) who do not belong to the 'ethnic minority' categories. If we include all persons born abroad living in the UK, irrespective of colour and citizenship, but do not consider the further demographic impact of their children, then we obtain a similar figure although it includes a partly different set of populations. In 2000, according to the Labour Force Survey, the total number of overseas-born persons in the UK was 4.6 million (7.8 per cent of the population) and the number of foreign citizens (which excludes immigrants who were British and the large number who have naturalised) was 2.9 million (4.9 per cent of the population). The similarity between the ethnic minority total and the foreign-born total is partly co-incidental—membership of these two categories is somewhat different. Unlike the continental situation, persons born in the UK to legal foreign residents have normally been treated as British citizens. These numbers are likely to be under-estimates because immigrants, especially from third-world countries, are known to have higher rates of non-response to surveys and censuses than ordinary citizens.

A different picture is given if immigration is considered irrespective of origins and citizenship. For example, if it were assumed that there had been no net migration at all in the period 1950 to 2000, then the net effect is more modest, because the net inflow of persons of foreign origin at all times (which increased population) is partly counteracted by the net outflow of British citizens until 1982, which diminished population, other things being equal. Some simulations of the UK population from 1951 to 2000, made by Youssef Courbage and Paul Compton,[12] show the net effect if there had been no net migration either way in any year, compared with the actual outcome with migration. Their analysis shows that, from the 1980s onwards, the rate of population growth without migration would have flattened out. With migration, an accelerating growth has resumed. The net effect of the latter scenario was to add 1.35 million persons, of all citizenships including British.

Despite the emphasis made by the present government on the supposed economic and other benefits of migration, it has made no reference to the effects on overall or regional population size. The effect on London and the South-East has been particularly profound. By the 1960s London's population had stabilised and was declining, partly assisted by a government policy of reducing population density by encouraging out-migration to the 'new towns' such as Swindon. Since the late 1980s, London's population has grown rapidly—partly through international migration and partly through the continuing high fertility of many of the ethnic minority populations in London. Ken Livingstone, the Mayor of London, has produced a pamphlet extolling the merits of this growth as an example of London's economic dynamism.[13] Its projections of London's population are sharply upwards, from 7.4 million today to over 8.1 million by 2016, with even more substantial projections for household growth and housing demand.

Official projections of the UK population issued by the Government Actuary's Department (GAD) now assume substantial future annual net flows. The GAD population projections based on 2000 assume a net immigration of 135,000 each year until 2050, with a high variant of 195,000 and a low variant of 75,000.[14] The actual net figure for 2000 was, of course 183,000 on the previous basis of calculation. Successive projections from the GAD, necessarily cautious, have been several tens of thousands below the actual figure for over a decade. That in the 1998-based projection was just 95,000; until the 1996-based projection a decline to zero net immigration was assumed. A separate Home Office publication[15] has projected net immigration, of foreign citizens, from outside the EU only, rising to just under 180,000 by 2005. Calculations based on net immigration of 185,000 rather than the GAD's 135,000 point to an increase of 11 million; from today's 60 million to 71 million by 2050.[16] In both cases, the increase is mostly due to international migration. The 2000-based population projections from the GAD indicate an increase in the UK population of 4.1 million by the year 2021. Population projections based upon the base population and the migration estimates dictated by the 2001 census (58.8 million and 100,000 respectively) indicate a UK population of 62.4 million in 2021. This is 1.7 million fewer than in the 2000-based pre-census projection total; an increase from 2001 of 3.6 million compared with 4.1 million.[17]

Effects on the age-structure

As far as the age structure is concerned, so far the effects, analysed by Compton and Courbage,[18] have been modest, amounting to not more than a three per cent addition to any one age-group. This is in line with the results of previous work.[19] There is no evidence here of any marked 'rejuvenation' of the age-structure. The effects are more potent on the total population size and even more on its ethnic composition.

Population ageing and 'replacement migration'

The effects on the age structure bring us to the concept of so-called replacement migration. It has been widely stated, partly thanks to a UN report,[20] that Europe 'needs' very large numbers of additional migrants to save itself from its own geriatric future, to make up for the babies which Europeans will not have, to stimulate the economy, and so on. The UN performed some rather ingenious calculations which showed that if Europe wanted to preserve the present size of its population of working age on present trends, then it would need to import millions of persons every year into the foreseeable future, assuming that the birth rate did not return to the replacement level. If Europe wished to preserve its present 'support ratio'—the ratio of the population of working age to the retired population—and thereby preserve itself from population ageing, then it would have to import very many more immigrants: up to 14 million new immigrants every year for the foreseeable future, with spectacular effects upon population growth.

The problem of population ageing is general in the whole Western World. It is a fundamental consequence of low birth and death rates. Any modern population, which enjoys an expectation of life of (let us say) 75 years, where family size is controlled at the average of two or less, is bound to acquire a permanently different age structure from that in which we live now.

Today's age structure was inherited from the twentieth century and was created by its vital rates. It is unstable and non-sustainable. The only way in which it could be preserved into the future is by cutting back expectation of life to about 50 years, by persuading the average family to have at least three and a half children, or by importing rather large numbers of immigrants.

Today the potential support ratio (PSR: the number of people of potential working age, nominally 15 to 64, for every person of retired dependent age, normally over 65) stands at just over four in most European countries. That is not the real ratio of actual workers or taxpayers to retired dependants, which is much less (about 2.5 to 1). Only about 64 per cent of Europeans aged 15-64 are at work.

In the future it is likely that the potential support ratio will go down to not more than two and a half, and in some countries not more than one and a half, depending mostly upon the future level of the birth rate. The official GAD 1998-based projection of the potential support ratio for the UK until 2101 is given in Figure 2 (p. 23).

Like all projections it will go wrong, but possibly not too badly wrong. On its assumptions of mild increases in survival and in fertility, with 95,000 net immigrants, the PSR falls from about four to about two and a half. Figure 3 (p. 24) shows the likely future in other European countries on current assumptions: France, the UK, Germany, Italy and Spain. All begin with a PSR of around about four but decline to different levels: over two in the case of France and the UK, well under two in the case of Germany, and in the case of Italy and Spain, less than one and a half (1.36 in Spain). These results suggest quite big differences in future prospects for the economy, productivity, dependency, and other indicators. The two different projections for the UK arise because the assumptions made by the GAD and the UN are not the same.

Cannot these problems be solved with more immigrants? The answer is 'yes' only if astonishing levels of population growth can be contemplated, with the consequent eventual demographic marginalisation of the current population. Figure 4 (p. 25), derived from official calculations,[21] shows the population size consequent on the migration needed to preserve the current potential support ratio in the UK up to 2100. Today's population of 60 million would have doubled to 120 million by 2050 because the UK would be importing

Figure 2
Potential support ratio, UK 1998 - 2101

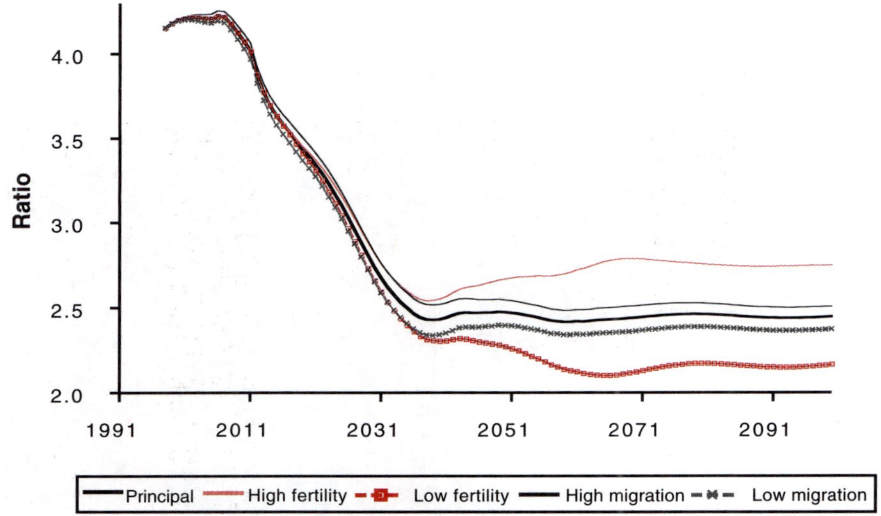

Note: Some senarios omitted for clarity.
Source: Unpublished calculations by Government Actuary's Department

Figure 3
Potential support ratio, selected countries, 2000, 2050

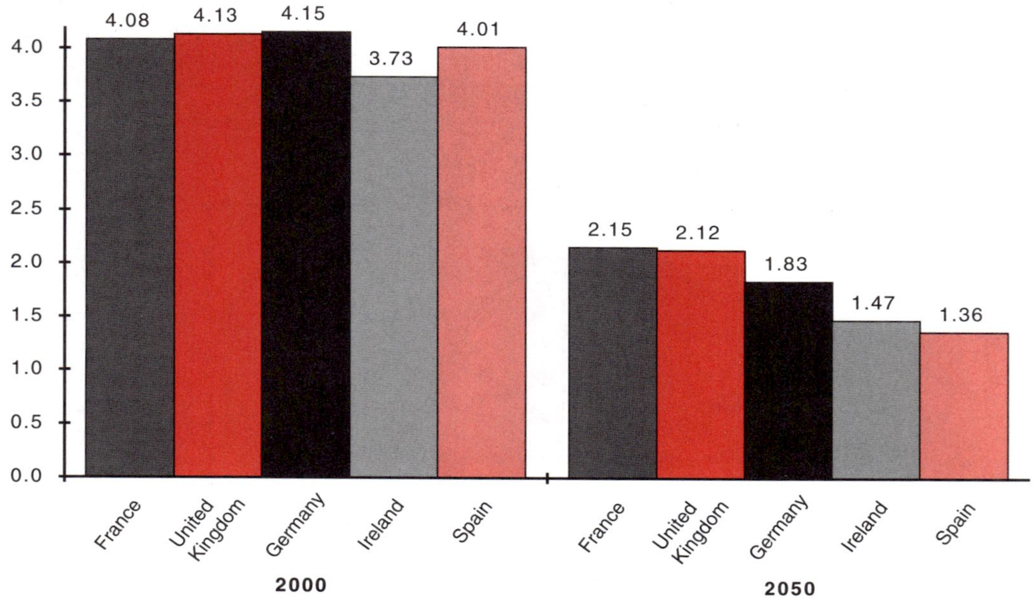

Source: United Nations 1998-based population projections

Figure 4

Population size required to maintain given PSR by immigration, UK 1998-2100, given fertility and mortality rates as in the GAD 1998 principal projection

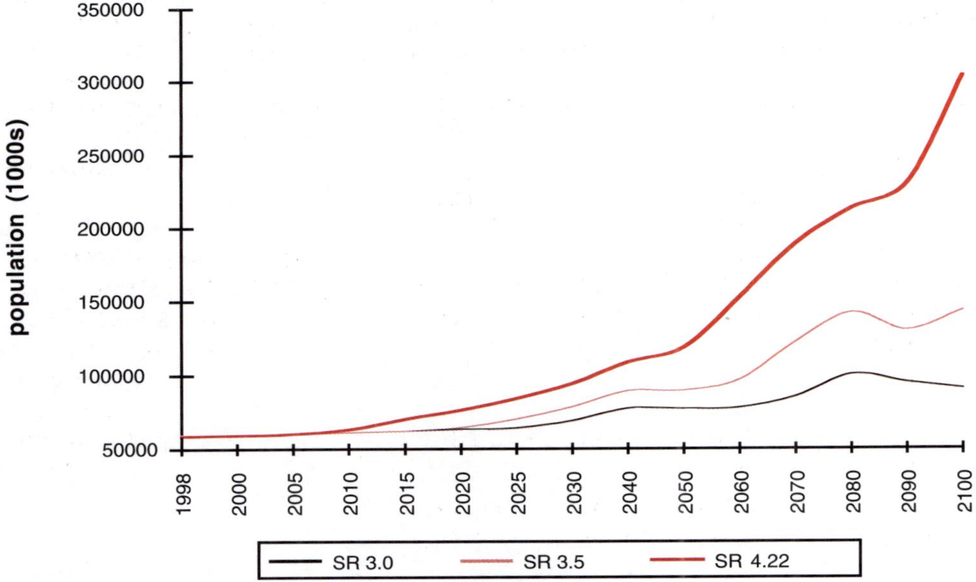

Source: Unpublished calculations from the Government Actuary's Department

Table 2
Comparison of UK scenarios at 2050 by order of potential support ratio

Projection	Total population	Median age	Percent aged 65+	Support ratio	Working age limit
	Values in 2050				
(Actual 1998)	59.2	36.9	15.7	4.15	62.5
Constant 1998 vital rates	64.2	42.7	20.4	3.12	68.3
TFR=2.07	71.8	40.4	21.7	2.75	70.6
TFR=2.07, high e_0	72.6	40.9	22.4	2.64	71.5
185k constant migration	70.6	43.4	23.2	2.61	71.1
TFR=2.07, zero migration	63.1	41.6	23.2	2.53	72.1
GAD 1998 Principal Projection	64.2	44.1	24.2	2.47	72.0
TFR=2.07, high e_0, zero migration	63.9	42.2	24.0	2.42	73.0
TFR=1.7	61.7	45.5	25.2	2.38	72.6
High e_0	65.0	44.6	25.1	2.37	72.8
Zero migration	56.1	45.8	26.0	2.25	73.6

Note: Except where specified, all scenarios employ the same assumptions as the GAD 1998-based Principal Projection:
TFR rising to 1.8, constant migration of 95,000 per year, expectation of life rising to 79.7 and 83.9 years for males and females respectively by 2060. The 'working age limit' is the corresponding formal retirement age 'required' to preserve the current potential support ratio of 4.1. e_0 is expectation of life at birth, both sexes.
Source: unpublished calculations by UK Government Actuary's Department

1.2 million persons per year. By 2100, up to five million new immigrants would be needed every year, and the population would have risen to 312 million, not much less than the present population of the whole EU.

The *reductio ad absurdum* of all this is what one might call the 'Korea syndrome'. It concerns the level of immigration required in order to preserve the current potential support ratio in the Republic of Korea, and its consequences for population growth. In order to preserve the present potential support ratio of Korea—10:1, better than ours—the population would need to increase to 6.2 billion people by the year 2050. Just by coincidence, this happens to be the entire population of the planet at the present time.

It would not do to pretend that immigration does not have a favourable impact upon the age structure. The problem is that the effect is not very great and immigration is an inefficient way of achieving this end. Immigrants themselves age and then require more immigrants, as it were, to replace their number. Also, there is a tendency for immigrant birth rates to converge to those of the host population, although by no means a complete one. Population ageing is a consequence of low birth and death rates, not of a failure of migration: birth rates are a much more effective way of changing age-structure. It must be made clear that population ageing cannot be 'solved' by fertility either, although it is easier to moderate it by that route. Even if the birth rate rose up to replacement level, the support ratio would only increase to about 2.9. But that would imply no further population growth and eventually, with constant mortality rates, an end to further population ageing. To keep the PSR at four, a family size of three and a half would be required.

Table 2 (p. 26) shows this in the UK case. This contrasts the consequences of 185,000 incoming migrants per year—the present volume of net migration—with the effect of the birth rate going up to 2.07. That is the so-called 'replacement rate', the rate which will maintain the population to a constant level, and a constant age structure, over the long run and with zero migration.

With today's lower birth rate (here assumed to be 1.7), and about 185,000 migrants per year, the result is a slightly more favourable support ratio than with replacement fertility (2.07) and with zero net migration. On the other hand, that advantage is paid for with the penalty of a considerably bigger population, with almost 7.5 million extra people by 2050. Free market liberals may feel that population growth is not a penalty, but a benefit. This is arguable, but since the UK is a densely populated island, not facing decline for decades, there seems no obvious need for even more population, and many argue for the benefits of a smaller one. At the end of the day, population growth—British, European and global—must cease eventually.

Effects of immigration on the workforce

What are the consequences of immigration for the workforce? The net inflow of employed foreign persons was only about 50,000 a year even in 2000 (Table 3, below), perhaps surprisingly in view of the government's recent policies. While there has been an increase in the number of workers arriving under work permits, there has always been a very substantial flow outwards. In most years during the 1990s, the International Passenger Survey shows that the same number, or even a larger number, left Britain for purposes of work as entered it for purposes of work. The recent announcement of a record 175,000 work permits for the coming year must make for a net positive inflow, however.

Table 3
UK foreign workforce 2000:
basic characteristics of stocks and flows

Foreign workers (citizenship)	1.039m	3.9%
Foreign workers (birthplace)	2.190m	8.2%
Work permit gross inflow 2000	86 thousand	-
Net inflow of employed foreigners 1999	46 thousand	0.2%

Source: Dobson, Koser, McLaughlan and Salt, *International Migration and the United Kingdom*, 2001.[22]

As far as the distribution is concerned, Table 4 (below) shows the distribution of the workforce by nationality. No major section of the economy (Table 5, below) has an overwhelming preponderance of foreign workers. At this simple level of analysis by sector of economic activity it is apparent that there is no striking level of segmentation or concentration in the work force, or dependence on foreign workers, although this can be seen at local level or in more finely-defined occupational areas.

Table 4
Distribution of British and foreign workers by industry (percent)

Industry / activity	**British**	**Non-British**
Primary	5	3
Manufacture, Building	23	17
Distribution, Hotels, Catering, Repair	20	21
Finance and Business	14	16
Transport, Communication and other services	39	43
Total	100	100

Source: Dobson *et al*, 2001.

There are some particular occupations where immigrant populations are concentrated and statistically over-represented (Table 5).

Table 5
Over-representation of foreign workers in given sectors

Construction
Transport
Administration
Finance, Information Technology
Other services especially Medicine
Clothing manufacture
Wholesale and retail
Hotels and restaurants
Posts and telecommunications

Source: Dobson *et al*, 2001.

In the UK the National Health Service has been partly dependent, for the last 30 years, on overseas labour in the form of doctors and nurses recruited from India, the West Indies and other parts of the world. These make up perhaps 30 per cent of personnel. This dependency is unique in Europe and unusual anywhere in the industrial world. Another under-funded nationalised industry—teaching in state schools—is also finding that it must recruit overseas, partly in order to meet the demand for teaching accentuated by growing immigrant and asylum populations in the South East and London. This solution is evidently not without its problems.[23] In the private sector there is considerable demand for IT specialists which, it was claimed, can only be met by overseas recruitment, from India, and elsewhere, which is shared by most of the rest of the developed world. However, so transient has this demand proved that IT posts were removed from the Government's list of occupations in short supply in 2002.

But in general, ethnic segmentation in the work force is not very marked. Pakistanis, Bangladeshis and West Indians tend to be concentrated in lower-grade jobs (restaurants and transport) and among the unemployed, but Indians and East-African Asians are over-represented in high status occupations (medicine and finance) and their social status is higher than that of the average English person.[24] In the UK at least there are no 'dirty jobs' (sweeping, refuse collection) which are the exclusive occupation of foreign workers, although some enthusiasts for migration insist that it is exactly for these occupations that low-skill foreign immigration is needed. Illegal employment of foreigners in some occupations is becoming marked, however, for example office cleaning (Africans) and prostitution (Eastern Europeans), most of them illegally resident. With the possible exception of medicine, no major sector of the British economy is dependent upon migration in, for example, the same way that tourism is dependent upon it in Switzerland.

Fiscal benefits and costs of migration

When all the sums are added up, does immigration emerge as a net economic benefit or cost? Few doubt the advantages to employers, and probably to the economy, of the ability to recruit highly-skilled workers to fill job vacancies. In the past, the majority of workers coming to Britain under work permit were highly skilled, although they comprised only a small proportion of all immigrants. But this labour migration is a two-way process—in most years in the 1990s just as many left the UK for work as entered for work. And most immigrants are not workers. It is the overall effect—taking into account all immigration—that matters.

Many analyses of the net economic effects of immigration to Europe, especially those done during the 1960s guest worker period when most immigrants were workers, came to unequivocally favourable conclusions.

As time has gone on, and as the pattern of economic demand and of immigration flows and immigrant populations have changed the conclusions have become more nuanced and in some cases negative. The important sectors of the economy now demand more skilled or professional workers; European economies have moved on from their need for the semi-skilled metal-bashers of the guest worker era. The majority of legal migrants to the UK, and to Europe, and also to the United States, over the last two or three decades, did not enter primarily for the purposes of work. They have entered as dependants, as students, as new spouses for the growing immigrant populations in the case of Europe or more recently as asylum claimants. Only a minority has entered through any job-recruitment process.

Computing the exact benefit when many immigrants are not workers is obviously difficult: for example the US National Research Council[25] concluded that all immigration (legal and illegal) to the US might add as little as $1 billion and as much as $10 billion per year to the US economy which was then growing at $400 billion per year. That is, immigration might contribute as little as 0.25 per cent to the rate of growth or as much as 2.5 per cent. More certain is the fact that immigration was then adding about 0.5 per cent per year to population and comprised about 60 per cent of population growth. If the lower end of the economic growth estimate is taken, immigration was making the average US resident slightly poorer in the 1990s.

In the United States, economic benefits and costs from migration have been shown to depend upon whether state or federal taxes and welfare are considered. George Borgas's recent book *Heaven's Door*[26] concluded that more recent immigrants to the United States contributed much less to the economy than in previous decades, partly because of a declining skill level, and that their presence might well disadvantage poorer American workers. Danish research has shown that while immigrants from rich countries are economically beneficial to Denmark, those from poor countries impose a net cost.[27] Recent Swedish research seems to suggest that overall, the net economic effect of recent immigration has been negative, pointing out that more recent migrants tended to be much less well-equipped in terms of capital and also much more prone to be unemployed. Research in the UK cannot reach such comparably precise conclusions. The UK lacks the person-number registration system, which in Denmark, Sweden, and Norway can provide exact information on taxes paid and benefits and health care received by individuals.

Very little work on this had been done in the UK since the 1970s,[28] partly because UK economists considered that the economic effects of migration, either way, were too trivial to worry about. However, with much higher immigration rates, and a government keen to talk up and stoke up immigration, things are changing. For example, the Home Office, in alliance with a left-leaning think-tank, the Institute for Public Policy Research (IPPR), have jointly produced studies pointing out the merits of migration.[29] While carefully done, these studies are limited, employing only easily accessible conventional statistics and ignoring difficult areas even when relevant statistics are available. According to one of these publications, the fiscal contributions of immigrants, in a rather broad sense, in 2000, were about £31 billion. The costs were about £29 million; the advantage being £2.5 billion (Table 6 p. 33).

If the results of this UK study are taken at face value, the £2.5 billion fiscal gain from immigration comprises just 0.25 per cent of the 2000 UK GDP of £944.7 billion. While this does represents growth in overall GDP, the important consideration is whether the average income per head of population is thereby increased. Immigration increases the population as well as the GDP. A simple calculation shows that the net contribution of net immigration to UK population growth in 2000 (0.31 per cent) is actually slightly greater than the contribution of immigration to net GDP growth (0.25 per cent). On the report's figures alone, even if taken at face value, GDP per head is apparently diminished as a consequence of immigration (the factor of population growth is not mentioned anywhere in this or any other of the government's recent reports).

Table 6
Immigration to the UK:
fiscal and workforce efficiency

Fiscal efficiency	
Immigrant fiscal contributions 1999/2000	£31.2bn
Immigrant fiscal costs 1999/2000	£28.8bn
Fiscal advantage	£2.5bn

Source: Gott and Johnston, *The Migrant Population in the UK: Fiscal Effects*, 2002, p. iii.

However, the report's statistics cannot be taken at face value; they omit too much. The report explicitly assumed that the costs for immigrants and natives alike in relation to education, crime, prisons and public disorder were exactly equal. This is known not to be the case. Ever since the 1960s, special additional expenditure, for example the Home Office's Section 11 grant, has been directed at schools with high proportions of immigrant pupils to overcome problems of poor English and other handicaps. Schools in London, for example, now have to cope with 150 different languages. For decades, considerable sums have been earmarked for specific ethnic projects, and more generally for the urban regeneration of areas where immigrants concentrate, through the government's Urban Programme and its successors. Ethnic minority households are more likely than average to be in poverty.[30] The proportion of immigrant and ethnic minority population has been for years a component of the official indices of need used to channel public money to local authorities through Revenue Support Grant.

The disproportionately large involvement of ethnic minority youth in robbery, burglary and drug-related crime is attested by statistics from victimisation surveys, convictions and imprisonment:[31] ethnic minority youth has been responsible for over half the street crime in London for decades, and has been the focus of intermittent but destructive riots. The causes of all this are controversial, and many of these problems do not involve immigrants but their children. The Home Office will have easy access to relevant statistics but has chosen to ignore them. More widely, the report also does not consider the loss to the UK economy through the considerable sums sent home by immigrants as remittances, the increase of which has nullified a previously favourable balance, and the great sums spent on the asylum process—officially over £1.7 billion in 2001/02. Not much change, therefore, out of the '£2.5 billion'.

Economic activity of immigrants in the UK

Economic activity includes both those who are employed, and those who are unemployed, but actively seeking work. Immigrants typically are younger than the average age of the populations into which they move and a higher proportion of immigrants are therefore of working age. However, this does not necessarily mean that the workforce participation rate—the proportion economically active in the population of working age (conventionally 15-64) or even of all ages over 15—is actually higher among immigrants than among the general population. For example, a recent major study[32] showed that in the UK 64 per cent of British citizens aged 16 and over were economically active in 2000, compared with the 59 per cent for the foreign population (Table 7, below). Looking at the population of working age, between 16 (the minimum school leaving age) and 60/65 (the current retirement ages for women and men respectively) we see that 80 per cent of British citizens in those age-groups were economically active in the year 2000 compared with 69 per cent of the foreign population. Unemployment was also higher among the foreign population: 8.5 per cent compared with 5.5 per cent. The position with regard to the ethnic minority population—which numbers four million and includes citizens and non-citizens and both immigrants and their children born in the UK—is less favourable. In almost all groups, unemployment has been higher and workforce participation rates lower, particularly among Bangladeshis and Pakistanis: just 50 per cent in 1999. Only a minority of women in these populations work, being confined to domestic duties and the raising of what are often large families.

Table 7
Workforce participation and unemployment

	By citizenship, 2000	
Economically active	UK (%)	Foreign (%)
All ages over 16	64	59
Ages 15-59/64	80	69
Unemployed	5.5	8.5
	By ethnic minority status, 1999	
	Economically active (%)	Unemployed (%)
White	80	6
All ethnic minority	66	13
Black	73	15
Indian	71	9
Pakistani/ Bangladeshi	50	19
Other	66	12

Source: Dobson *et al*, 2001; *Labour Market Trends*, 2000.

Unemployment is typically twice as high as the native level; a similar situation is found among foreign populations in other Western European countries (where 'ethnic minorities' are usually not defined).[33]

Social and political consequences

No comprehensive review has ever been attempted of the social and political consequences of large-scale migration to the UK. Diversity—an American term never used until about ten years ago—was originally assumed almost axiomatically to be a problem, not something to celebrate, requiring a difficult process of acculturation or assimilation on the part of immigrants. The official and establishment view is now firmly that the multi-cultural diversity arising from immigration, especially from non-European immigration, is culturally and socially beneficial and should be protected and preserved through various multi-cultural policies, and that it is the duty of the host society to adapt to it. This new orthodoxy is promoted by the Commission for Racial Equality, and a pervasive range of publicity measures from the Home Office Race Relations and Diversity Unit. A pervasive 'anti-racist' education programme has been proposed, to which all elements of school teaching should adhere (Race Relations [Amendment]Act 2000, Qualifications and Curriculum Authority 2003).[34]

Yet the cultural benefits to be celebrated are more often proclaimed than listed and indeed seem rather difficult to specify beyond a wider range of ethnic restaurants for the middle classes and new kinds of pop music for youth. Critics of multi-cultural policy and the diversity which it seeks to perpetuate, however, claim that it helps to preserve the isolation and segregation of immigrant populations and the accentuation of new social divisions in Western society with the potential for serious conflicts of interest and of loyalties. 'Diversity' adds a new and relatively intractable set of social divisions, including the novelty of caste, on top of the unsolved and well-known social class divisions from which the UK has traditionally suffered. Communities are now divided by language and custom in new ways. Contradictions have arisen between traditional modes of behaviour and attitudes and those customary in a modern democracy, for example on the role of women in society and the education appropriate to them, a separation of church and state, tolerance of indifference to religion and of sexual unorthodoxy. Cultural traditions of some immigrant minorities may hamper their social advancement and economic progress in a British setting—the predominance of lone-parent families among West Indians, for example, and of single-earner households and large family size among Pakistanis and Bangladeshis.[35] While some groups such as Indians and East African Asians have risen well above the national average in professional level, education, and income, others still fall below it. Bangladeshis and Afro-Caribbeans still tend to be concentrated in lower-level jobs, have less success in school and high levels of unemployment

Table 8
Proportion of births to mothers born overseas in selected major cities, 1999

England and Wales	14%
Greater London	39%
Inner London	49%
Birmingham	26%
Bradford	27%
Oldham	23%

Source: Office for National Statistics, *Birth Statistics 2000*, Series FM1 No. 28, London: The Stationery Office, 2002.

In 2000, the interesting question of ethnic replacement was raised in the national press: whether the high rates of immigration, and the relatively high level of fertility in some immigrant groups would cause Britain to cease to be numerically a white country. Speculation by a black political activist that this might come about even before the end of this century was first reported in the *Observer*, a respectable Sunday newspaper. While it is true that the current relative growth rates of the white and non-white populations might point in that direction if they remain unchanged, birth rates are expected to converge and immigration is at least nominally under state control and can go down as well as up. No national projections by ethnic origin have been made since 1979,[36] although new ones are being prepared by the ONS and by academics.[37] Informed comment will have to await their appearance. Whatever happens nationally, ethnic displacement is becoming a reality in many large cities. Local authorities in cities such as Leicester and Bradford already project non-white majorities in a decade or two, and it is inevitable in many London boroughs and probably in London as a whole, the former now confirmed by the 2001 census.

Most members of immigrant and ethnic minority populations get along with fellow Britons quite well and the spread of friendships across racial and ethnic lines, increasingly taken for granted, is underlined by the growth of inter-ethnic unions. Nonetheless, the political consequences do not seem to have been very favourable and tensions and problems remain especially at the 'group' level. The events of September 11 and the responses to them have revealed a hitherto undiscussed security problem, in the disturbing level of sympathy for al-Qaeda and its aims revealed by some opinion polls among young Asians in Britain. This general problem is actually of longer standing. Under Conservative and Labour governments, numerous terrorist activists have been granted refuge in London, which has acquired an unenviable reputation among some foreign governments as a terrorist haven. Until very recently the authorities seem to have ignored the persistent and blatant incitement to acts of violence and religious and racial hatred arising from clerics in various mosques in the UK, presumably for fear of disturbing 'race relations'.

In order to advance the interests of immigrant and ethnic minority populations and to diminish the undoubted prevalence of discrimination, a pervasive apparatus of ethnic monitoring and enforcement has been created over the years. Group rights, enjoyed by minorities alone over and above individual rights, are now widely recognised. Ethnic origin is now required to be stated in applications for almost all public appointments, grants and other services, even to the extent of gaining planning permission for house extensions. Quotas, nominally illegal but thinly disguised as 'targets', are widely imposed for recruitment and promotion. The Race Relations Acts permit certain kinds of positive discrimination in favour of minorities, in training, in the public subsidy of 'black housing associations' and elsewhere. As the 2001 census asked a question on religion, primarily at the insistence of ethnic minority groups, we may expect to see this apparatus extended to religious belief as well. This transformation of the United Kingdom into an ethnically corporate state providing group rights for some over and above individual rights for all is of dubious constitutional propriety and has never received democratic sanction. Such practices and 'group rights' are explicitly rejected as divisive and counter to the principle of the equality of citizenship in some other European countries, notably France.

Resistance to these policies is very difficult. Objection to the more pro-active 'anti-racist' elements of multi-cultural policy is now regarded as *prima facie* evidence of racism. That epithet has been widely used to quell spoken and printed opposition or criticism of immigration and of the immigration process. All problems encountered by immigrant populations are by definition caused by the racism and discrimination, direct, indirect or 'institutional', of the host society. These issues are policed and investigated by the Commission for Racial Equality, which has extraordinary powers to investigate the actions and even the motivations of institutions and individuals. In the course of all this Britain appears to be in the process of being turned upside down, particularly in respect of policing and criminal justice and immigration control, by inappropriate reactions to tragic individual ethnic victims and the demands of pressure groups.[38] Censorship and self-censorship prevails in these areas among academics, publishers and some of the national press. Some newspapers will not publish articles critical of the pro-immigration establishment consensus. Issues such as ethnic minority involvement in crime are generally off-limits.

This is not a healthy state of affairs when opinion polls consistently show that a majority of the public feel that immigration is excessive but where all the main political parties now favour a multi-cultural line and none has a clear policy to attempt to moderate regular migration flows or radically to reform asylum, integration or multi-cultural policy.

Conclusion

This analysis has taken a rather pessimistic view of the overall effects of international migration, in its current large-scale form, on the UK. In part this is in critical response to the exaggerated, unrealistic and uncritical praise directed at its effects in the last few years. It should be remembered, however, that (most) immigrants themselves are not responsible for any adverse consequences of large-scale migration. Migrants seek to improve their lot and that of their families. For the most part the motivations of those coming to Britain are similar to those which have sent several million Britons overseas from the seventeenth century onwards. The problems of immigration are not the fault of migrants but are consequences of a British failure: the failure of our political system to moderate migration flows in the first place, and the subsequent failure to establish firm and just principles and mechanisms whereby those coming to Britain might be encouraged to accommodate themselves to the society in which they had chosen to settle.

Immigrant integration— the American experience

Tamar Jacoby

Immigrant integration—or absorption or assimilation—is an old and familiar story in the United States. So much so that one of our greatest historians, Oscar Handlin, began his greatest book by declaring: 'Once I thought to write a history of the immigrants in America. Then I discovered that immigrants *were* America's history [and that to tell their story fully would require] setting down the whole history of the United States.' The immigrant experience is also an intimate story for most people in the US. We're almost all the children of immigrants, and we all know something of 'the melting pot'.

Yet, for all this, it is instructive to come to Europe and compare notes with those of you here who are also dealing with issues of immigration and immigrant absorption. The metaphor that comes to my mind is two people commiserating outside a clinic. Not that immigration is necessarily a complaint or an illness. On the contrary, in the right number and under the right circumstances, immigration is a great boon to the receiving country—to its economy and its spirit. But the influx does sometimes come with some aches and pains, and plainly many of our countries are facing those aches and pains today.

The good news is that assimilation is going pretty well these days in the United States. It is true that this is a much disputed and much monitored question—and rightly so. After all, with over a million legal and illegal immigrants coming into the country every year, if they're not assimilating, we're heading for real trouble. But most of the evidence I see supports a degree of optimism.

Obviously, the first component of absorption is economic. It's not the be-all and end-all. You can be doing all right economically and still not be fully integrated. But it's certainly the first building block. And as I read the economic data, on this score, the glass is at least half full.

Most immigrants who come to America come to work. Most don't get welfare—they are not entitled to it for the first five to ten years. They know from other immigrants who have preceded them from their regions whether or not work is available. Communications are very good now between American cities and the little villages of Latin America. If there aren't many jobs to be had, few immigrants make the trip. After all, if you're going to be unemployed, it's much better to unemployed at home than in the US. It's usually a lot warmer at home and much less expensive to live, and you're usually surrounded by a network of supportive family and friends. So even though, technically, three-quarters of American immigrant visas are given out on the basis of family ties, almost every foreigner who comes to the US gets a job—or two or three jobs—and works hard at it. Indeed, Hispanic males—and Hispanics account for about half the foreign-born in the US—have the highest labour-force participation rates of any group in the country.

Now of course it's true that many immigrants are poor and the jobs they do are often the dirtiest and most dangerous jobs—jobs that native-born Americans don't want to do, like busboy and chambermaid and assembly-line worker in a meat-processing plant. But these people at the bottom of the economic ladder are only one component of the vast flow of immigrants that has come to America in recent decades. The US has also accepted a lot of people at the top end of the economic ladder such as nurses, engineers and entrepreneurs. About a quarter of today's newcomers have less than nine years of schooling, but another quarter have university degrees. And when you mix this second group's educational background with the phenomenal personal drive most immigrants bring, it can prove an unbeatable combination. Just spend some time in Silicon Valley, where foreign-born scientists account for a third of the scientific workforce and Chinese and Indian entrepreneurs run a quarter of the high-tech companies.

To be sure, the poverty and social backgrounds of many of today's newcomers are a cause for concern. There's no question that, like many European nations, the United States today is basically a middle-class country importing a new lower class. America no longer has a lower class, and it turns out that it needs one. And even this doesn't necessarily mean the newcomers aren't going to be absorbed by the economy or do well by it, because generally they do. In fact, by the time the average immigrant has been in the US for ten or 15 years, he or she is usually making more than the average native-born American.

Which brings us to the second component of integration: how are the immigrants' children faring? This is a critical question. After all, the first generation is always transitional. They always live between two worlds, and if they arrive as adults, they never fully integrate. And to some degree, in America today, it's too soon to tell how the second generation is doing. Nevertheless, the evidence is beginning to trickle in, and to me it looks a lot more positive than negative.

Troubling signs do exist. Those who were born abroad—or whose parents were—often start at the bottom of the socioeconomic ladder. They certainly go to some of the worst schools in the country—failing, overcrowded inner-city schools, where many of the native-born students disdain learning and scorn mainstream success. And yes, some second-generation immigrant kids catch this bad attitude from their schoolmates.

But, as a group, these immigrant children come home with a superb record card. One important study[1] conducted over the last decade in San Diego and Miami found that, whatever country they come from, across the board, they work harder than their native-born classmates. They do an average two hours of homework a night compared with the 'normal' 30 minutes. They aspire to greater achievement than American-born students. They get better grades, and they drop out far less often—between a third and half as often. So if school performance is any guide, we need not worry: today's second generation is likely to outstrip its parents educationally and economically, vindicating the parents' urge to take the risk of coming to the US to make a better life for their families.

The third key component of assimilation is language. Are today's immigrants learning to speak English? This is an issue of huge concern in the US—it is probably the greatest fear of those who worry that assimilation is not working—and there is no question, there is a lot more Spanish in the air today than there used to be 20 or 30 years ago. There are signs in Spanish just about everywhere you go. Politicians from heavily immigrant areas are falling over themselves to learn Spanish. Even corporate America is catching the bug, spending hundreds of millions of dollars a year on advertising in Spanish and even Mandarin Chinese. So it would be easy to surmise that immigrants are not learning English, particularly not Hispanic immigrants, who often live in large enclaves of other Spanish-speaking people, where, some argue, you do not need English to get by.

But in fact, it turns out that the conventional wisdom driving people to campaign and advertise in Spanish is quite wrong. According to the Census, about ten per cent of the US population now lives in a household where Spanish is spoken. That sounds like a fairly large number but it's misleading, because for the Census Bureau, even one Spanish speaker—and in many cases, it's an elderly grandparent—is enough to get a family classified as Spanish-speaking. And within those households, 85 per cent of the kids and 70 per cent of the working-age adults speak English well or very well.

This has nothing to do with language classes. America doesn't provide much in the way of language classes. It's mainly about the power and reach of American pop culture. About 60 per cent of today's new immigrants come to the US speaking English well or very well—it's hard to avoid it in the world today, even in a poor village in rural Mexico. Despite the travesty that is bilingual education, virtually everyone who grows up in America eventually learns English. And according to the second-generation study,[2] by the end of high school, 98 per cent of today's immigrants' children speak and understand English well or very well, and nine out of ten prefer it to their mother tongues.

Still another indicator of assimilation is home-ownership—a fairly telling sign, after all, that you're putting down roots and investing in them. And here too, today's newcomers seem to be doing fairly well.

True, as those who are pessimistic about assimilation are quick to tell you, many recent immigrants are anything but settled. They go back and forth to the old country. They often leave their families at home and maintain strong ties to the old world. Still, after a while, they generally settle down. They ask their families to join them or they marry someone they've met in America, and within 20 years, 60 per cent of them are homeowners. And by the time they've been in the US for 25 years, they're actually more settled than native-born Americans—a significantly higher share of them own their own homes.

Similarly, with citizenship. True, today, unlike in the past, it is possible for people from many countries to maintain dual citizenship—and with it, perhaps, troublingly dual or conflicting loyalties. Naturalisation is also a slow, gradual process, and among those who arrived in the years since 1990, less than ten per cent have become citizens. Still, among those who have been in America since 1970, as many as 80 per cent are naturalised. If you stay, it turns out, you eventually join: today, as in the past, you eventually graduate from sojourner to member.

Finally, perhaps the ultimate measure of assimilation, there is the ethnic intermarriage rate—and in America today, it is simply stunning. Just to give some perspective, until very recently the black-white intermarriage rate was well under five per cent. But, when it comes to US-born Asians and US-born Hispanics, between a third and a half marry someone of a different ethnicity. And by the third generation, according to some demographers, the rates are over 50 per cent for both groups.

Naturally, none of these measures really capture that ineffable that is the essence of integration—the sense of fully belonging in a new land and a new culture. Do today's immigrants feel they are truly Americans? Do they place their loyalty to the things we all share as a nation above their loyalties to their groups and their particular ethnicities? Well, the sad truth is, relatively few people do, even among the native-born. The mainstream culture hardly encourages it. Many Americans themselves no longer know what it means to be American. Our schools teach at best a travesty of American history, distorted by political correctness and the excesses of multiculturalism. And, even in the wake of September 11, few leaders have tried to evoke more than a fuzzy, feel-good enthusiasm for America.

So there's no question that today's immigrants are at a disadvantage compared to yesterday's when it comes to what some people call 'patriotic assimilation'. But this is as much the nation's fault as it is the fault of immigrants. America is full of self-styled ethnic 'leaders', ethnic-studies professors and ethnic marketers fomenting chauvinism and divisiveness—most of them second- or third- or fourth-generation. Yet your average, hard-working immigrant is only baffled by identity politics. Today's migrants, like yesterday's, want to make it in America, not to live apart in anger and alienation. Their children may be a different matter and we may have to reach out to their children in a different way. But given half a chance, there's no one more patriotic than a new immigrant. You should have seen the flags flying in the Mexican-American neighbourhoods in the wake of 9/11. And according to one of the largest and most comprehensive national surveys of Latinos, conducted in 1999 by the *Washington Post*, 84 per cent believe it is 'important' or 'very important' for immigrants 'to change so that they blend into the larger society, as in the idea of the melting pot'.

So, to summarise, I think it is clear: today's newcomers are not spawning a new 'rainbow underclass'. Many of them are poor, most are struggling, they and their children face significant obstacles. But by and large, the immigrant integration story that's developing in America today is a success story. If you have any doubts, just spend some time among the Mexican-American middle class in a place like Houston, Texas, or with the first-generation Chinese-Americans—and there are quite a few of them—who sit on the board of overseers that runs the California state university system.

The question is what can be done, whether here in Europe or in America, to encourage and assist immigrant integration. But before I get to that, I want to look briefly at the parallel—or, more precisely, what is parallel and what isn't—between America and Europe. Certainly, Americans have been dealing with this issue for a lot longer. This does not mean that we are necessarily better at it: people tackling a question for the first time often bring a combination of energy and ideas that's missing among people who have been grappling with a problem forever. But certainly, there are some factors that make this issue a little easier in America.

It helps that there really is no such thing as a hereditary American in the way that there are in effect hereditary Frenchmen and hereditary Germans. America has always been a place where foreigners could show up and participate —maybe not on an equal basis, but still participate—and in most cases, they eventually found they were accepted as full members. It's also helps that we don't have—and never have had—an established religion. So neither your religion nor your ethnicity is an *a priori* obstacle to integration.

Comparing the current situations in Europe and the US, Americans are fortunate that the group that happens to be coming in the largest number, Latin Americans, have a long tradition of cultural and biological mixing—what they call *mestizaje*. The quintessential feature of the culture they come from is the way it blends Spanish and Indian and, in some cases, African elements. So they mix easily and comfortably, and in this, they're very different from Muslims, who make up a much larger share of the immigrants in Europe and who come from a very different tradition and often have a different attitude toward assimilation. Finally, unlike in Europe, crime is not a particular problem among American immigrants, and even in these relatively sour economic times, the unemployment rate in the US is nothing like unemployment rates in Europe.

There are a lot of ways in which I think we have it easier. And it's quite possible that the differences between the two continents make the American experience largely irrelevant in Europe. Still I think there are some general lessons that can be drawn from America's long history of immigrant absorption.

Immigration policy ought to be based on work

The primary criterion for who to let in ought to be who is coming to do a job that needs doing and that native-born people don't tend to want to do. Humanitarian concerns will inevitably have some effect on policy. Family reunification has a place and so, of course, does helping refugees. But the main reason people move from one country to another is to improve their lot, usually economically, and the only real, enduring interest a foreign country has in accepting them is if they're going to contribute. So let's recognise this and make it the basis of policy.

Besides, the more of a premium a country can place on economic migrants—the more clearly it can acknowledge those who are economic migrants and the more access it gives them to its labour markets—the better immigrant integration will work. People who work establish roots and relationships. People who work learn the language. People who work eventually better themselves. And people who work earn the respect of their fellow countrymen. For all our history of immigration, Americans too sometimes lose sight of this, and our essentially family-driven system sometimes gets us in trouble because of the way it's out of sync with our labour needs. But if anything, the principle seems even more relevant here in Europe. Why not recognise that whatever the political circumstances in countries like Turkey and Afghanistan, many of the migrants from those places are coming to Europe to work and make a better life for themselves? Recognise this, let them work

—and reap the rewards, as working helps them to assimilate.

Too much government assistance is a mistake

Refugees who for one reason or another cannot work may need some help from the government. But this isn't true for most economic migrants—and for them, assistance can be as much a curse as a blessing. All too often, welfare discourages work and the assimilation that inevitably comes with it. In the case of government housing, whether in accommodation centers or elsewhere, the supposedly helping hand of the state encourages segregation. Too warm a welcome creates a false incentive for other would-be migrants, luring more people into the country than can productively work and integrate there. And it only leads the native-born to look down on the migrants who receive it, further adding to the difficulty of assimilating.

Of course, all of this begs the question: how much is too much? And I'm not against providing some basic services—whether emergency services or other necessities—as well as any assistance that helps spur assimilation. I'm all for better public schools, for example, and vocational apprenticeships and classes that help people learn to help themselves—teaching them financial literacy and that sort of thing. I also support allowing even illegal immigrants' children to go to public universities—a controversial issue at the moment in the United States. But I don't think the US made a mistake in barring immigrants from receiving welfare, and to the degree that's possible in Europe, I urge you to consider it.

Short-sighted, unrealistic laws that force otherwise legitimate migrants to live underground are only going to slow their absorption

This is only common sense. The law-abiding are more likely to fit into society and be accepted there than people who live outside the law and adopt the habits of law-breakers. The problem in the US is that although a million immigrants come into the country each year to work, the law only recognises two-thirds that number—and the other third are forced to sneak in and then to live like fugitives. Not only does this criminalise badly needed productive activity, it also makes an ass of the law—and creates all kinds of obstacles to assimilation. And I'm sure this must be true in Europe too, where so many who want to work are forced to work illegally, and even those seeking asylum often start their new lives as outlaws. If they are going to come anyway, far better to recognise reality and create legitimate channels.

It is not a mistake to make demands of immigrants

Demands that they learn the language in their new, adopted country; demands that they learn the manners and mores; demands that they eventually become citizens. This is not racist or unduly nationalistic, although this sort of incorporation effort should be as positive as possible—a matter not of sanctions and punishment but of highlighting the allure of the new country. You ask and encourage people to learn the ways of a culture because those ways are the keys to success there. And if you're going to require, say, learning the language, you ought to provide and pay for classes. (At the very least, even if the government won't provide them, it ought to create incentives so that others do.)

Don't ask people to obliterate their old loyalties

America does not ask immigrants to forget about their ethnicity. On the contrary, anyone who knows what makes America great knows that Italian-Americans will be Italian, Jewish Americans will be Jewish—and in the twenty-first century, Latino-Americans will be Latino. What we ask—or have asked in the past—is that people learn to balance the two sides of their identity—the ethnic side and the American side. Traditionally, what this meant for most groups was that at home, on the weekends and in your neighbourhood—i.e. in private—you lived your ethnic background, or were free to. But when it came to the workday or the workplace or anything public or official, you were a citizen among citizens and you could be accepted as a full member there in the public sphere, no matter what you did or were at home.

It's true that this traditional balance is somewhat out of kilter in the US today. Our obsessive and insistent multiculturalism has disrupted the age-old equilibrium. We may not be requiring enough of our new immigrants—or holding out enough in the way of a coherent idea of what it means to be American. And this is a crucial challenge for the US going forward.

But immigrant absorption cannot work without this balance, because you can not expect people to simply give up who they are—to throw away the habits they have grown up with and the age-old loyalties that help to make them strong. But you also can't hope to assimilate them unless you permit and encourage full membership. So—and this is the bottom line—you have to come up with a notion of membership that allows for some kind of hyphenated existence that isn't second-class. At least that's the formula in America.

The great question, of course, is whether any of this can work in Europe. I don't think there's any doubt that it is what has made America what it is today. From British political traditions to Jewish humour, from the German work ethic to Irish eloquence: just about everything that makes America great was brought there by an immigrant. But Europe is a very different place, with little or no tradition of immigrant absorption and where people are already anxious that for one reason or another—globalisation, modernisation—the traditional fabric and character of the society is being eroded. It is easy to understand those concerns and to see why immigration poses a harder challenge there.

In the long run, however, it's a challenge that cannot be avoided. For demographic reasons, because of changing labour needs, thanks to globalisation and the ever-accelerating inter-connectedness of the world today: immigration is Europe's future whether she likes it or not. Better to recognise it, regularise it, bring it above ground—and get on with the hard business of helping the newcomers assimilate.

Immigration and the labour market: a Spanish perspective

Juan José Toribio

Spanish immigration policy is based on a law passed on 11 January 2000. Despite its youth, this law is now subject to vigorous discussion in Spain. A significant degree of political discussion revolves around reforming the law and the development of a new immigration policy.

The problem of immigration is a recent one for Spain. It has traditionally been a country with a high level of emigration: to the former American colonies and, in the 1960s, to the rest of Europe. However, things have changed radically in recent years and Spanish society is now contemplating, with some apprehension, a phenomenon to which it is not accustomed.

Spanish immigration law considers legal Spanish residents to be those who have obtained either a temporary or permanent residence permit. The temporary residence permit, which allows stays of over 90 days and less than five years, is granted to all foreigners who can guarantee that they will have sufficient financial means to support their living costs, and where necessary those of their family, during the period they have asked to stay in the country.

Permits are also granted to those who intend to do business, for themselves or for others who have obtained administrative authorisation to work. This group would also be entitled to bring their family to Spain.

To summarise, for any person who wishes to have a temporary residence permit in Spain, for between 90 days and five years, one of the following three conditions must apply:

- To have their own economic means and be able to prove it
- The bringing together of the family
- To have obtained a permit to work in Spain.

The first condition does not pose a problem. In fact, for many foreign residents, especially Europeans who decide to live in Spain after retirement, the only thing they have to do is to demonstrate that they have an adequate pension or sufficient means to live on.

The second condition is fairly restrictive: only children and parents but not other relatives may immigrate to Spain.

The third condition for obtaining a residence permit is to have a permit to work in Spain. A work permit can be obtained if the applicant fits within the quota of foreign workers, which is fixed annually. This quota is determined by the leaders of the regional governments who recommend the number of work permits that can be given in the different economic sectors to central government, by means of a body called the 'Superior Congress for Immigration policy', through which the opinions of trade unions and employers' associations are expressed, and finally, by means of a decision from the government.

If you wish to obtain a work permit in Spain, it is best to start being patient now, as it is not simple for all these conditions to coincide to prove that you are worthy of a Spanish work permit. Of course, if you were to obtain a work permit in Spain you would be able to renew it every year as long as you continued to fulfil these conditions and at the end of five years you would automatically become a permanent resident of Spain. You would be able to do the same jobs as any Spanish citizen, or any citizen of the European Union, who has, by definition, the same right of access to jobs as the citizens of the country in question. You would not necessarily have the right to vote, however, and you would not have the right to work for the Spanish government.

Protected by all this administrative complexity, or in many cases, ignoring it and therefore breaking the law, there are more than a million foreign citizens resident in Spain at this moment.

Spain has a population of 40 million people. Foreign citizens thus account for between 2.5 to 3 per cent of the total Spanish population. Not a very high proportion, compared to Canada, Australia, New Zealand or the United States, but one which is rapidly increasing. Of this million, approximately 320,000, or one third, are citizens of the European Union, and therefore are not considered foreigners for employment purposes. Some 70,000 are foreigners from other European countries and the rest, that is to say, two thirds, 600,000 are from other non-European countries.

By country, the highest proportion of immigrants in Spain comes from Morocco. According to the statistics, approximately 250,000 to 300,000 Moroccans reside in Spain at this moment; this is slightly less than a third of the entire foreign population. Certainly, a very large proportion of these citizens go to the Spanish cities of Ceuta and Melilla, in North Africa, so a relatively large proportion of those Moroccans live in these two cities, but they also live in the rest of Spain. And curiously, quite a large proportion of these Moroccan residents gain access to Spain with the status of European citizen, offering as proof of eligibility that they are relatives of other Moroccan citizens who live in other countries of the European Union. After Moroccans, the next largest group of foreigners in Spain comes from Latin American countries such as Ecuador, Colombia, Peru and the Dominican Republic. There is also a relatively large body of Chinese immigrants.

This raises the country's first point for political debate—whether this distribution of nationalities, supposing it were a model for future immigration, is satisfactory or not for Spanish citizens. Certainly, the proximity of the country of origin explains why Moroccan immigration is proportionally so large in our country. Nevertheless, almost all questionnaires completed by Spanish citizens show that the majority of the Spanish population would prefer immigrants to come from countries, which although racially diverse, maintain a cultural, ideological and historical affinity with Spain, so that the social integration of the immigrants would be easier. These questionnaires are not very different to those which can be found in France and the United Kingdom, where it appears that people also tend to be in favour of people from the former colonies, who at least speak the language of the country.

The largest number of immigrants in Spain live in Catalonia, where the issue of immigration is causing some of the most pressing political problems of the moment. Quarter of a million immigrants live there out of a population of six million. The community of Madrid has just over 200,000, that is to say, a little less than in Catalonia, though the community of Madrid has a smaller population of five million people. After that comes Andalucia, and of course the Balearic Islands, the Canary Islands, Ceuta and Melilla. But the northern regions of Spain, such as Cantabria, Asturias, the Basque Country and Galicia, have a much lower percentage of immigrants. Hence, the intensity of discussion surrounding the issue of immigration varies a great deal depending on the region.

If we also consider the fluctuation in immigration in recent years (which can be worked out by differences in the size of the foreign population from one year to the next) we observe how the flow of immigrants into Spain has increased in an extraordinary manner since 1996-97. Curiously this has happened simultaneously as employment has increased in Spain and at a time when productivity in Spain was falling. Evidently, this flow is accelerating at the moment and it is estimated that around 100,000 - 120,000 legal immigrants will enter the country per year. It is much more difficult, naturally, to calculate the flow and quantity of illegal immigrants. Some estimates reckon that the number of illegal immigrants now resident in Spain could be between 200,000 and 300,000.

The periodic legalisation of illegal immigrants, by giving them the status of legal residents of Spain, even though they would not otherwise have fulfilled the conditions, is always undertaken by governments with the promise that this will be the last time they will carry out such a process.

They said this in 1985, 1991, 1996 and again in the year 2000. Consequently, the percentage of legal immigrants who live in Spain, who were originally 'illegal', is far from negligible.

This process creates several problems. Some have already emerged, such as penal law. Others, especially economic consequences, are still subject to a lively discussion.

The United Nations places Spain among those countries most likely to experience a relative decline in population during the next 50 years. Assuming that there is zero immigration and taking into account the low fertility rate and the increase in life expectancy, estimates predict a drop of ten million people. The current population of 40 million would become 30 million by the year 2050, a fall of approximately 25 per cent.

Also, in accordance with other much less reliable estimates and taking into account the likely change in productivity, we can assume that Spanish GNP will fall by around 15 per cent in the next 50 years. This probable reduction of the Spanish population will only be surpassed in its intensity by Italy, which predicts a fall of 28 per cent, and some of the former Soviet bloc countries, such as Bulgaria, Romania, the Czech Republic, Slovenia, Hungary and certain Baltic Republics. However, Spain is amongst the countries with the highest probable decrease in population.

Spain is not only amongst the countries with the highest probable decrease in population but also among those with the highest possibility of an ageing population. It is estimated that the population will have aged most in the next 50 years. At the moment, approximately ten per cent of the world's population is over 60 years old. However, in Spain this figure is 22 per cent. In 2050, in accordance with a simple extrapolation of the current trends, more than 20 per cent of the world's population will be older than 60, but in Spain a massive 45 per cent of the population will, it seems, be older than 65.

There are, then, sufficient economic arguments to propose a more open immigration policy. It is argued that immigration could hold the answers to this problem of the decrease in and ageing of the population. First, the population could be boosted by the sheer number of immigrants, simply because they exist. Second, because they tend to be a younger population and therefore could reduce the problem of the rate of dependency. Finally, because the fertility rate among immigrants seems to be higher, although it does not need to be very high for it to be higher than that of the current Spanish fertility rate.

So what effect will immigration have on jobs and salaries in Spain? We must first take into account that Spain has the highest rate of unemployment in the European Union. Clearly, this would seem to be a decisive factor in the formation of a future immigration policy. However, this would not, in my judgement, be a good idea.

Time and time again, this high Spanish unemployment rate distinguishes itself as the factor that should guide our future immigration policy and as a factor that justifies the current enormous administrative complexity surrounding the issue of work permits. The argument can reach ridiculous extremes. For example, in the community of Madrid and of course in Spain generally there are many thousands of families trying to legalise a domestic help who has emigrated to Spain illegally, who is fulfilling an important economic function, at least for the families in question, and who is not taking anyone's job away from them. After requesting their legalisation over and over again, you will most probably receive a reply from the administration saying that, because it has been agreed that in this sector there is unemployment (it is unclear where the statistics come from) you do not have the right to legalisation. This could happen whether you were talking about legalising a waiter, a hairdresser or any other profession.

The stance of the Circulo de Empresarios (Madrid's Business Round Table), and my own, is that the problem that confronts us is much more a problem of liberalisation of the labour market than a problem of the limitation of immigration. Unemployment in Spain is not caused by immigration; unemployment in Spain is caused by the rigidity of the labour market. We must take into account, however, that when we talk about the labour market and the impact of immigration on employment and the level of salaries, in the end, jobs are just one of the production resources. The price of production resources is determined not only by the fluctuation of these resources, in this case, immigration, but also by the fluctuation in services capital. When we try realistically to analyse what the effect of the fluctuation in immigration on salaries and jobs might be, we will never achieve a clear answer because we would need to take into account the fluctuation of capital and the fluctuation in goods and services.

The other key point of discussion in Spain concerns social protection for immigrants. Spanish law gives immigrants the right to education, if they are completely legal, and if they are illegal, a right to education if they are 18 or under. All foreigners who come to Spain have the right to health care whether they are legal or illegal. They have rights to housing, although it is not clear how to put this into practice, at least for those who are legal. Legal immigrants have a right to social security, pensions and other social rights, although the law adds that illegal immigrants also have access to the basic services and benefits. Nobody defines, however, when a service or benefit is basic and when it is not, and the end result is that there is a great deal of debate about what services immigrants are actually entitled to.

One can conclude, then, that Spain is a country that will have serious demographic problems if it does not open itself up to immigration. One can also conclude that the problem of immigration is, nevertheless, a European problem. After the Schengen agreement it is absurd that immigration policies should continue to be a national concern, as immigrants can enter through any of the borders of the European Union. Therefore, we should have a common European policy on immigration in which Spain should participate very actively, if for no other reason than because it is so close to the African continent, which constitutes a gateway to Europe for a large proportion of immigrants.

Spain needs to contribute to the European Union a resolute drive towards democratic capitalism, free enterprise and the fight against protectionist forces and, therefore, to facilitate immigration in greater quantities. We recommend a greater flexibility of the Spanish labour market, and also a revision of the whole welfare system, where the problems, which are falsely attributed to immigration, truly reside. There is a need to respect the law and see to it that immigration is extensive. Spain should be a country open to immigration and at the same time demanding legitimacy of these immigrants.

This opens other alternatives such as the education of these so-called immigrants or potential immigrants in their own countries and of our country's more active participation in co-operative programmes with non-EU countries.

What we propose is a more reasonable, more open immigration policy focused more on the authentic economic needs of the country and a reform of the internal structures of the labour market and the welfare state in order to be able to admit the surge of immigrants that Spain will, without doubt, need in the next few years and that Spain will inevitably get in the next few years whether we want it or not.

Numbers and national identity

Robert Rowthorn

Hardly a day goes by without some major item in the British media about immigration: police batter down the door of a mosque to deport a family whose application for asylum has been rejected; illegal immigrants are asphyxiated in the back of a van smuggling them into Britain; there is a running conflict with the French government over the question of illegal immigration through the Channel Tunnel; the government relaxes the rules for skilled immigrants and temporary workers, but tightens controls on asylum seekers; the Home Secretary, David Blunkett, announces new requirements for citizenship; he also calls on immigrants from South Asia to find marriage partners for their children in Britain rather than bring them from abroad; following race riots in the North of England the British National Party gains seats in the local council elections on an anti-immigration platform. Similar stories abound elsewhere in Western Europe.

Migration is a highly contentious issue. It involves many conflicting interests and raises difficult moral and practical questions, especially for the inhabitants of rich countries such as ours. How many immigrants should the rich countries admit and according to what criteria should they be selected? By what means should the flow of immigrants be controlled? What responsibilities do we have to those who are kept out and to their mostly poor countries of origin? Indeed, is it right or even necessary to restrict immigration in the first place? These questions are already the subject

I am grateful to William Brown, Ha-Joon Chang, David Coleman, Geoffrey Harcourt, Sriya Iyer, Paul Ormerod, Carlos Rodriguez, Ajit Singh and Amanda Wharton for their comments on earlier drafts of this paper.

of intense debate in many countries, and the debate promises to become even more intense in the future. In this paper I shall focus mainly on Britain, although many of my remarks will be of relevance to other rich countries, especially those in Western Europe.

Immigration[1]

A government minister recently declared that Britain is a nation of immigrants. This is misleading. Until the 1950s there had been no sustained immigration into Britain, other than from Ireland, since the Norman invasion nearly 1,000 years ago. About 100,000 Huguenots arrived from France in the seventeenth century. This is equivalent to about 1.5 per cent of the total population of England, Scotland and Wales at the time. A similar number of Jews arrived in the late nineteenth century and approximately 70,000 refugees from Nazi Germany were admitted in the 1930s. These inflows are equivalent to 0.4 per cent and 0.2 per cent respectively of the host population. Sustained immigration dates back only to the 1950s, when migrants from the Caribbean and South Asia began to arrive in Britain. Many of that generation of immigrants are still alive today.

Racial tension led to successively tighter restrictions on immigration, and by 1971 it was believed that primary immigration had been brought to an end. The government accepted that immigrants could bring other family members into the country, but this was thought to be merely a transitory phase. Once this phase was over, the ethnic minority population would stabilise at a modest level, and the main policy challenge would be how best to integrate them into British society.

These expectations turned out to be false. According to official statistics, the net inflow of foreigners into Britain was 182,100 in the year 2001.[2] This figure excludes 20,625 dependants of asylum seekers together with a substantial, but unknown, number of illegal immigrants.[3] When allowance is made for these exclusions, the true figure for net foreign immigration must be well over 200,000. Even 200,000 is seven times the total number of Ugandan Asians who arrived in Britain following their expulsion by Idi Amin in 1972. It is equivalent to more than two million per decade. Some of these immigrants are labour migrants who enter the country for explicitly economic reasons. Others are asylum seekers and their dependants, or spouses for the descendants of Asian immigrants. Even where immigration is ostensibly for some other purpose, there is often an economic motive. For example, economic migrants may falsely claim to be asylum seekers, while genuine refugees from a poor country may fail to go home when the danger is past because they are better off in Britain. Following a marriage between someone from Britain and someone from a poor country, the couple will normally choose to live in Britain where economic prospects for them are much better.

There is also fertility to consider. Most immigrants are relatively young and many come from cultures where large families are the norm. As a result, the birth rate amongst immigrants is on average higher than amongst the native population, in some cases much higher. This further boosts the number of immigrants and their proximate descendants. The combined impact of immigration and fertility can be gauged from official statistics on what are called ethnic minorities. Over the five-year period, 1992-4 to 1997-99, the ethnic minority population grew by 15 per cent.[4] For Bangladeshis and Black Africans the figures were 30 per cent and 38 per cent respectively. The number of people classified as mixed-race rose by 36 per cent, reflecting the high rate of interbreeding between certain ethnic minorities, especially Black Caribbeans, and the white population. If immigration were to be severely curtailed, then within a few generations much of the existing ethnic minority population would be assimilated through interbreeding with the rest of the population, although some particular subgroups, such as Muslim Bangladeshis, might remain fairly separate for a long time.

The native population

To decide who belongs to the native population of Britain is not easy. How many generations must we go back, and what proportion of foreign blood disqualifies someone from inclusion as a native? Even though the rate of immigration has been low for most of our history, if we go back a few centuries, most people now alive in Britain have at least one foreign-born ancestor. Since I am concerned with the impact of post-war immigration, I shall define as a native any current inhabitant of Britain who is neither a post-war immigrant nor the descendant of such a person. Thus, a couple who entered the country before World War II are classified as native British and so are their children. This is not an ideal definition, but no reasonable modification would seriously affect the argument.

A striking feature of the native British population is its failure to reproduce. Following the baby boom of the immediate post-war decades, the birth rate of the native British fell considerably and their total fertility rate is now around 1.55. This is above the figure in some Southern European countries such as Italy, but it is well below the level of 2.1 that is required to maintain a stationary population. As a result, the number of native British of childbearing age will soon begin to fall and this trend may accelerate as the echoes of the post-war baby boom fade away and the population ages.

Social composition

Through a combination of immigration and differential fertility, the composition of the British population has altered considerably over the past 50 years. First generation immigrants now constitute around eight per cent of the population. What will happen to this figure in the future depends on a number of factors, some of which are amenable to government policy and others are not. If immigration were to continue at the rate observed over the past three years, then by the middle of the century about one in seven of the population would be foreign-born. This is higher than the share of first generation immigrants in the United States today, which is often cited as the model we should imitate.[5] Many of these immigrants would be white, although a majority would belong to some other ethnic group. The cumulative impact of immigration on the size of the ethnic minority population in Britain would depend on both the number of immigrants and their reproductive behaviour. There are no official statistics on the ethnicity of migrants and this must inferred from data on their geographical origin. Such data suggest that, over the past three years, the net immigration of people from ethnic minorities has averaged about 100 thousand per annum. With immigration on this scale the ethnic minority population, including people of mixed race, could reach 20 per cent of the national population by 2050.[6] Given the uncertainties involved, one should treat this projection with caution, but even so it does indicate the orders of magnitude involved. It is much higher than the current ethnic minority share of 7.8 per cent in the national population.[7] With a more restrictive entry policy the ethnic minority population would grow more slowly and a greater fraction of this population would be of mixed race or have British-born parents. There would also be fewer white immigrants.

An important issue in this context is immigration from the poorer East European countries, such as Poland. Some of these countries are due to join the EU in 2004 and others, including Turkey, may be admitted in a few years. At present, migration from such countries is restricted, but for those joining the EU next year Britain (unlike some other EU states) has said that they will be free to work in this country at once. This will swell the number of immigrants and make the task of containing immigration even more difficult than it is now. It will also lend an extra racial bias to the control of immigration. Light-skinned immigrants from some quite poor EU countries will be allowed in, whereas darker-skinned immigrants from other poor countries in other continents will still be kept out.

The statistics on Muslims in Britain are especially striking. They form a separate and fast-growing subgroup of the population, whose numbers are increasing rapidly because of immigration and their above average birth rate. According to one estimate, the number of Muslims has more than doubled over the past 20 years. Given the secular decline in church attendance, it is possible that by the middle of the century there will be fewer practising Christians in Britain than there are active followers of Islam and other non-Christian religions.[8]

In both scale and speed, the transformation that is now underway is without precedent. Britain is not alone in this respect. Many countries in Western Europe are undergoing a similar change in their ethnic and cultural composition through immigration and differential fertility, and in many of them the subject is forcing itself up the agenda just as it is in Britain.

Does it matter?

There are various reactions to the above developments. At one end of the spectrum are the extreme cosmopolitans, who view nation states and national identities as a dangerous anachronism, and would promote a comprehensive mixing of the world's population in the name of diversity. At the other extreme are the ethnic nationalists who wish to defend the purity of their own nation against all comers. My own position lies between these extremes. I accept that immigration on a modest scale brings benefits in the form of diversity and new ideas, but the pace of the present transformation in Europe worries me. I believe it to be a recipe for conflict. I also believe that nations are historical communities that have the right to shape their own collective future as they see fit, and to resist developments that undermine their identity and sense of historical continuity. I do not believe that nation states and national identity are dangerous anachronisms. Nor do I believe that they can, or should, be refashioned at will by a cosmopolitan élite to accord with its own vision of how the world should be. Many nations, especially in Europe, have deep historical roots and their existence promotes the kind of global diversity that cosmopolitans allegedly value. Many cosmopolitans accept the right of 'oppressed peoples', such as the Palestinians, to a homeland and an identity, but they regard such aspirations as illegitimate when expressed by the historic majorities of Western Europe.

European nation states are facing a challenge on many different levels. It is not just a question of immigration and ethnic transformation. Global economic developments in the realm of trade, production and finance have greatly undermined the former coherence of their national economies. Political developments are undermining both the sovereignty and the internal democratic structures of these nations. For example, supra-national bodies such as the World Trade Organisation, the European Commission, the European Court of Justice, the European Court of Human Rights and the European Central Bank, are constantly extending their powers into new areas and pre-empting or over-riding the democratic institutions of individual countries. It is not surprising that the political parties most hostile to immigration are normally the most hostile to economic globalisation and to supra-national institutions. They are raising, albeit in xenophobic form, issues of community, identity and self-determination that should be of concern to all democrats.

History, community and identity

Benedict Anderson has used the term 'imagined community' to describe a nation. Some writers have interpreted this term as synonymous with 'imaginary' and, by implication, unreal and easily malleable. But this is false. A nation is no more imaginary than a language. Indeed, they are similar and related entities. Both have an abstract, symbolic dimension that establishes a connection between people who do not personally know each other. Both have historical roots and, once established in the minds of the people, take on a life of their own.

A nation is a community and as such is to some extent exclusive. Its members share a sense of common identity and have special moral obligations to each other. The national community also has moral obligations to outsiders, although these are more limited than towards its own members. Not everyone in the community will share this sense of national identity and moral obligation in the same way or to the same extent. Some people may hardly feel part of the nation at all because they are too self-absorbed or too cosmopolitan in outlook. Some people may identify strongly with certain features of the nation, but not with others. But these differences do not matter as long as there is enough common ground to give the nation coherence and preserve a sense of historical continuity. Notice that I am talking about identity and the moral obligations that are associated with it. These are not legal concepts, although they may have a counterpart in the laws with regard to citizenship and its rights and responsibilities.

A nation is a community of mutual obligation that is based on a shared history. This is captured by the well-known aphorisms: 'A nation which does not look after its own is no nation'; and 'A nation without a past is a nation without a future'. Or as Cicero warned, 'cultures without history doom themselves to remaining trapped in the present, akin to small children who know neither whence they have come nor whither they go'. Members of a national community have special moral obligations to each other, to future members and to those who are dead. As Burke said, society is a compact between the living, the dead and the not yet born. The existence of such a community is rooted in history, and history is a central component of its self-understanding.

Over the past 30 years, the notion of history as a grand narrative has gone out of fashion, and idea of placing the national history and culture at the centre of teaching in our schools has been attacked as ethnocentric and reactionary. As a result, many British children leave school with no sense of the broad sweep of their national history and culture, and they feel neither pride in the achievements of their nation, nor shame at its wrongdoings. Indeed, they have little knowledge of either. There are various reasons for this state of affairs. One is a desire to provide children with a cosmopolitan education to fit them for our post-imperial and, by implication, post-national future. Another is the desire not to embarrass or exclude children from ethnic minorities by teaching them about events with which neither they nor their parents have any personal connection.

The latter reason supports my argument that numbers matter. If a country experiences mass immigration, then it will soon contain a very large number of people who have no personal connection with the quite recent past and feel neither pride nor shame about this past. Their connection with the distant past will be even more tenuous. What was previously the history of the nation may come to be seen as merely the history of a shrinking ethnic majority, of little relevance to the rest.

This was brought home to me recently by a poster advertising the Imperial War Museum at Duxford airfield near Cambridge. In this poster there is a young white boy running across a field with a spitfire flying just over his head. Underneath are the words 'Your history matters'. How long, I wonder, will it be before such a poster is banned because it seen as discriminatory towards the children of post-war immigrants, especially those from ethnic minorities? World War II is my history, because I lived through it. Via me it is also the history of my children. When we talk of the war, we automatically use the word 'we' to denote Britain and the British of that time. 'We fought the Nazis'; 'We bombed Dresden' etc. We are proud that, under Winston Churchill, our nation spurned the offer of peace that would have saved us in return for abandoning Europe to the Nazis. We are ashamed that our leaders could order the deliberate bombing of civilians in Dresden and other German cities. To the rational mind, this all this sounds very emotional, as indeed it is. But then, identity is an emotional thing.

The presence of ethnic minorities has made it more difficult to teach a coherent national history. However, this task is not impossible. Take, for instance, the Second World War. The Battle of Britain, as represented by the spitfire in the above example, was largely a white affair and it is difficult for children from ethnic minorities to identify with it in the way that my children do. But the war effort as a whole relied heavily on troops of all colours from all parts of the British Empire. Hundreds of thousands of Indians, Africans and Caribbeans served as volunteers in the imperial armed forces, sometimes with conspicuous bravery. Few British children, white or otherwise, are aware of this fact. Indeed, few of them know much about the Empire at all. As a result, they know little about the forces that have shaped modern Britain or about the historical ties between Britain and the countries from which many ethnic minorities come. The solution is not to abandon the teaching of a national history, but to set this history in a wider context. Children should learn about the intertwined development of our nation and its empire, about the eventual loss of this empire and the nature of the post-imperial age. Such a programme would have its dangers, of course. In the wrong hands, it could degenerate into a catalogue of Britain's real and imaginary imperial failings. But taught in a more balanced fashion, which included the positive as well as the negative aspects of empire, it could provide a unifying perspective that would be relevant to all British children no matter what their ethnic background.

The history of a nation is not transmitted simply through structured narrative. It is also embodied in a host of symbolic forms: the monarchy, flags, ceremonies, public events etc. These symbols and their significance are always in a state of flux, but if the pace of change is too rapid or in the wrong direction, the result will be disorientation and resentment. Let me give an example. The badge of the Metropolitan Police has always contained the British crown, to indicate that the police are formally accountable to the monarch as official head of state. A recruit recently objected to this on the grounds that, as a devout Muslim, he could not wear the crown because it is surmounted by a Christian cross. In response, the Metropolitan Police have agreed to produce an alternative badge without the crown. In itself, this may seem a trivial example, but there are many others and more are sure to come. What will happen, for example, if someone decides that our national flag, the Union Jack, is offensive to Muslims because it is composed of variations on the Christian cross? Will we have to design a new flag?

This may seem far-fetched, but it was only a few years ago that the Red Cross proposed getting rid of the cross because of its Christian connotations. The same organisation recently banned volunteers from displaying nativity scenes in its shops at Christmas because they might cause offence. This decision was criticised by the prominent Muslim peer, Lord Ahmed, who said that Muslims were used to co-existing with Christians and were not offended by such displays.

The response of Lord Ahmed differs sharply from the approach of modern secularists, who would suppress all visible manifestations of our country's Christian heritage if they could. On the pretext of avoiding offence and respecting diversity, they would drive Christianity out of the public arena altogether. They may claim to speak on behalf of the Muslims, but in fact the logic of their position is to suppress or marginalise all religions including Islam. In the name of diversity, they would create a bland public space in which no manifestation of religion was allowed for fear that someone might be offended. Implicit in Lord Ahmed's remarks is a quite different view of what diversity entails. The appropriate response is not to suppress our Christian heritage, but to accord to other religions more public recognition.[9] Instead of banning nativity scenes at Christmas the Red Cross should have encouraged its volunteers from other religions to mount shop window displays to celebrate their own festivals.

There are several reasons why such issues are coming to the fore at the present. One is the fact that the ethnic minority population is now quite large and is becoming more assertive. When numbers were very small, they had little alternative but to take things as they found them. As they grow in number, make progress in the society and become more confident, it is natural for them to demand a greater voice. Another reason has been the failure of our political élite to confront the issue of national identity and to articulate what kind of adaptation is expected on the part of newcomers and their children. For a long time, the very idea that newcomers should be expected to conform in some way was anathema in official circles, and the emphasis was almost exclusively on the need for change in the host society. However, official policy in this regard has recently begun to shift. There has been a belated recognition of the threat to national cohesion which immigration may pose if it is not properly handled. Our Home Secretary has recently introduced tougher requirements for citizenship, including knowledge of the national language and culture, together with a formal induction ceremony. Opinion polls reveal substantial support amongst ethnic minorities for these measures.

There are also signs of a popular backlash with regard to the issue of national identity. There has been an upsurge of popular interest in history, which is symbolised by the huge audience for Simon Schama's TV programmes that chronicle the history of Britain from the Stone Age to the end of the World War II. They describe both the shameful events in our history and those of which we can be proud. There have also been numerous other very popular TV series or individual programmes on specific aspects of our history, such as the Kings and Queens of England, the Civil War, the British Empire, Winston Churchill, etc. On cable television there is now a special channel devoted exclusively to British history. Quite apart from the interest in history, there has been an upsurge of popular enthusiasm for the symbols of national identity. Despite efforts in certain quarters to belittle their significance, the Queen Mother's funeral and the Queen's Jubilee attracted huge crowds. It has become once again respectable to fly the Union Jack, which has been reclaimed from the parties of the far Right.

In my opinion these developments reflect a reassertion of national identity by the historic majority of the country. However, they should not be equated with racism or hostility to foreigners. The most popular chronicler of our national history, Simon Schama, is the son of Jewish immigrants, and a well-known promoter of traditional English poetry is the black Caribbean immigrant and TV newsreader, Trevor MacDonald. The Queen has made a great effort to include the ethnic minorities in her Jubilee tour of the country, and the annual Remembrance Sunday service at the Cenotaph has been widened to include Muslim and Hindu representatives. One of the great social events of the nation is the Caribbean Notting Hill Carnival which attracts a huge multi-racial crowd. Two of the leading critics of European Monetary Union for its lack of democracy are the trade unionist Bill Morris and the Labour MP Diane Abbott. Both are black. The rapid growth of mixed-race couples both in real life and in TV soap operas also indicates that a reassertion of national identity does not imply hostility to people of immigrant descent. Indeed, many people of immigrant descent consider themselves to be British, and are regarded as British by most of the rest of the population.

The limits to immigration

There will always be a tension between universalism and particularism, between cosmopolitanism and nationalism. The problem is not to choose one or the other, but to hold these two poles in balance. A policy that devalues the history of a nation and undermines hegemony of its historic core will not in the long run serve the interests which cosmopolitans hold dear. The alternative to a world of well-defined nations is not a world of engaged global citizens working actively for the common good as the cosmopolitans imagine, but a world of isolated individuals and small groups, ruled at best by an élite of unaccountable illuminati, and at worst by authoritarians. It is better for humanity that the world is divided into cohesive, self-governing nations that respect and support each other, than for it to become a gigantic mixing pot that commands the loyalty of no one.

Some immigration is desirable in any society, but this must be kept within limits. What these limits are depends on the nation in question. In the case of Iceland, for example, there is little scope for immigration. The population is almost entirely descended from the original Norsemen who settled the island a thousand years ago, and this fact imbues the entire national culture and is central to Icelandic identity. Such a culture could not survive large-scale immigration. At the other extreme are the countries of white settlement, such as Australia, Canada, New Zealand and the United States. These are countries whose original population has been dispossessed by immigrants who have mostly arrived within the past two hundred years. Their immigrant intake has become increasingly diverse in recent times and so far they have been able to absorb newcomers on a much larger scale than most European countries. In the case of Australia, the official multicultural policy has facilitated rapid assimilation into the host society, rather than permanently segregate immigrant groups as some of its critics feared. However, one should be cautious in evaluating the future of these countries. All of them still have a European majority and it is hard to know what will happen if they become truly multi-ethnic states.

Most European countries lie between the two extremes. They are not as homogeneous as Iceland, but they are also not countries of recent settlement. Although some have significant immigrant and other ethnic minorities, they still have long-standing ethnic majorities that form the hegemonic core of the nation. In the case of Germany this core includes the descendants of post-war refugees from formerly German settlements in Eastern Europe. It is unrealistic to expect that the population of European countries will knowingly accept immigration on a scale that would transform them out of all recognition. Yet this is precisely what will happen if their governments heed the siren calls of those who claim that continued economic prosperity requires mass immigration.

The importance of numbers

The debate about immigrants is frequently cast in individual terms. Opponents often portray them as criminals or scroungers coming merely to prey on the local population or exploit the welfare state. In response, their supporters argue that most immigrants are honest and hard working, and desire merely to earn a decent living in a country that offers opportunities that are not available at home. On this point, the supporters are undoubtedly correct. Indeed, I would go further. Many immigrants are resourceful and ambitious, and the values of certain immigrant groups with regard issues such as marriage, care of the old or education are exemplary. It is often said that we should inculcate immigrants with our own values. I am always a bit uneasy when I hear this. What do we have in mind? Do we really want to replace Muslim collectivism by Western individualism? Do we really want Asian immigrants to shut away their old people in homes like we do, or to emulate our divorce rates?

When it comes to civic values such as respect for the law or free speech, I am not convinced that immigrants are on average worse than the native population. Islamic extremists may have a bad record in these areas, but they are not very numerous. Criminality may be relatively common amongst young Afro-Caribbean males, but this is no longer an immigration issue. There is now little immigration from the Caribbean, and most of the young men concerned were born in Britain, as indeed were many of their parents.

However, immigration is not simply a question of personal qualities. It is also a question of numbers. Rapid changes in the ethnic or cultural composition of a society may cause widespread disorientation, resentment and conflict. Even slow changes may lead to the same result if their cumulative effect is to undermine the position of a previously dominant group or a previously established *modus vivendi* between groups.

I first became aware of the importance of this issue some years ago when I co-authored a book on the conflict in Northern Ireland. When Ireland was partitioned in the 1920s, a new political entity attached to Britain was created, called Northern Ireland. Within this region, the Protestant population, who mostly supported the union with Britain, outnumbered the Catholic population, who were mostly nationalists, by a majority of almost two to one. However, the Catholics had a much higher birth rate and, if this had been the only factor, they would quickly have become a majority in the North and able to vote the region into a United Ireland. This did not happen in practice because Catholics emigrated in much larger numbers than Protestants, so they remained in a minority despite their higher birth rate. In recent years, the economic situation of Catholics has improved dramatically, in part because of equal opportunities legislation, and they no longer emigrate in large numbers. Indeed, emigration is now more common amongst Protestants. As a result, the number of Catholics in Northern Ireland is now increasing rapidly and quite soon the nationalists may enjoy the voting majority required to achieve a United Ireland. Thus, demography may ultimately win where insurrection has failed.

Another example, which has been in the news lately, comes from Wales. After a long period of decline, the Welsh language has in recent years shown signs of revival as a result of government support and broader cultural trends. However, this revival is now threatened by the large-scale immigration of English-speakers who are seeking to escape from urban life and enjoy the rural idyll of an unspoilt countryside. Welsh language activists are seeking government measures to restrict such immigration, although so far their pleas have fallen on deaf ears. The situation in Wales is very similar to that in Quebec, where the separatists fought a long and ultimately successful campaign to protect Francophone culture by controlling immigration into the province.

A final example comes from Kosovo. In 1950, there was a rough balance in Kosovo between births to Albanian Muslims and births to Orthodox Serbs. By 1996, the ratio was 4:1 in favour of the Albanians.[10] The Serbs were rapidly becoming an endangered minority. This transformation had come about partly because the Albanians had a much higher birth rate than the Serbs and partly because of Serbian emigration from the province. This is the demographic background that has been largely ignored in Western reporting of the conflict in Kosovo.

These are all extreme examples, but they do illustrate the point that numbers matter. Quite apart from its impact on social composition, mass immigration may also lead to an unsustainable growth in the total population of a country or region. The result may be unacceptable damage to both the natural environment and the quality of life enjoyed by the local inhabitants. It is a truism that population growth even at a slow rate cannot continue forever, and sooner or later must come to an end. This was the point made by the late Pim Fortuyn when he opposed further immigration because the Netherlands was already 'full up'. He may have been exaggerating, but the force of his argument cannot be denied. Within the space of a century, the population of the Netherlands has risen from five million in 1900 to 16 million today, and the country is now one of the most densely populated in the world. Moreover, the population is still rising because of continued immigration and the high birth rate of the existing immigrant population. Given these facts, Pim Fortuyn's concern about overcrowding does not seem unreasonable.

I often read that population growth is a good thing and hence there should be more immigration. This may be correct under particular circumstances, but as a general proposition it is surely false. No matter what its initial benefits, the time must eventually come when further population growth is undesirable. In the end it comes down to what is the optimum size of population? In most European countries, many people would agree that their population is already too large. This is certainly true in Britain. For us, population growth is now a cost not a benefit.

Some common arguments for mass immigration

Many advocates of large-scale immigration put forward the following economic reasons to justify their position. It provides a young workforce to support an ageing domestic population, it provides cheap labour to do the jobs that local workers are unwilling to perform, and it provides valuable skilled labour for the economy. On inspection, these reasons turn out to be highly questionable.

Replacement migration

Birth rates in the rich countries have been falling and people are living longer. As a result, the number of so-called 'working-age' adults per elderly person is in decline and it is becoming increasingly onerous to support the growing retired population. One widely canvassed solution is to import young immigrants to rejuvenate the ageing national population. This is known as 'replacement migration'. Such migration has a drawback that is not widely appreciated by the general public, but is familiar to professional demographers. Immigrants, like the rest of us, grow old. As they age, they will eventually leave the workforce and will no longer be available to support the elderly. On the contrary, if they remain in the country they will have to be supported by the next generation of workers. To rejuvenate the population through immigration requires not just a once-and-for-all influx of foreign workers, but a continuing flow of new immigrants in perpetuity. Once the flow stops, the natural process of ageing will take over, and the rejuvenating effect of past immigration will soon disappear. A country seeking to retain its youth through immigration is like the sixteenth century Princess Elizabeth of Transylvania, who sought to keep herself young by bathing in the blood of young maidens. Each bath appeared to restore her youth for a time, but the effect would soon wear off and she would then require another bath, and then another bath, and so on ad infinitum.

In a country where the birth rate is very low, immigration can prevent population decline. However, this level of immigration will not suffice to offset the effects of longer life expectancy on the age structure of the population. To achieve this result requires immigration on such a scale as to cause the population of the host country to explode. This issue has been highlighted in a recent article by the eminent Oxford demographer, David Coleman.[11] To preserve the present age structure of the 15 EU countries would require annual net immigration of 4.5 million by 2007 and seven million by 2024. In the case of Britain, to prevent the population from ageing would require the immigration of almost 60 million people over the next 50 years. By 2050 nearly 60 per cent of the population would consist of people who had arrived in the country since 1995 and their descendants. Such rates of immigration and population growth are out of the question. Coleman concludes that replacement migration at any feasible rate can have only a minor impact on the long-run age structure of Britain and other European countries.

Given that immigration on any feasible scale cannot rejuvenate European countries, the only option for these countries is to accept that the ageing of their populations is inevitable and to manage this process as best they can. The workforce should be augmented by raising the retirement age and finding jobs for the millions of Europeans who are currently unemployed, and people should be encouraged to save and invest more so as to cut the consumption of the young and raise productivity.

Guest-workers

Migrant labour is used on a large scale in some countries to perform jobs that are not very attractive to local workers. These include seasonal employment in agriculture and tourism, together with low status jobs such as cleaning. Much of this work is done by registered guest-workers who are supposed to go back to their country of origin when their temporary work permit expires. However, many guest-workers do not abide by this condition but remain in the host country as permanent immigrants. As one expert in the field, Phillip Martin, has quipped: 'There is nothing more permanent than a temporary migrant'. Guest-workers who remain in the host country require support in old age and their children contribute to the long-run growth of the population.

Thus, guest-workers can make a useful contribution to the host economy, but this should not be exaggerated. Some of these benefits depend on the fact that guest-workers will eventually return home, and such benefits will be lost if these workers settle in the host country. Moreover, if guest-workers do settle in the host country, their children may eventually gain an education and no longer be prepared to perform the same low-status jobs as their parents.

Skilled labour

Although restrictive in their attitude towards immigration in general, many rich countries are keen to attract skilled workers, business people and investors. The objective is to raise productivity and widen the tax-base so as to generate more revenue for the government. The benefits of such a policy may seem obvious, but there is also an important downside. Too much reliance on immigrants to supply skills and the like may remove the incentive to educate the domestic population and develop its entrepreneurial capacities. However, suppose we grant that the immigration of skilled workers and business people is of economic benefit to the host country. Does this make it a good thing? The answer depends on what view one takes of morality. To raise and educate a skilled worker requires a large investment of time and resources by taxpayers and family members in the worker's country of origin. When such a worker emigrates, the benefits of this investment will be mostly lost to the country of origin. Some money may filter back in the form of remittances to dependants left at home, but it will be the host country that receives most of the benefit. Skilled immigrants may increase production and generate tax revenue in their host country, but the counterpart will be lower production and less tax revenue in their country of origin.

Whilst the economic benefits of importing skilled migrants are often real, they may also be highly dubious in moral terms, especially if the sending country is poor. Many of the benefits to the host country are achieved at the expense of other countries, and represent little more than the expropriation of investments made by taxpayers and families in the rest of the world. What looks like a welcoming and unbiased immigration policy may conceal an unrequited transfer of valuable personnel and resources from poorer countries. Nowhere is this more obvious than in the case of medicine. Faced with a shortage of doctors and nurses, our National Health Service has been recruiting staff from all over the world, including many poor countries that cannot match the kind of salaries available in Britain. According to the *British Medical Journal*[12] more than 3,000 nurses and midwives have left Nigeria, South Africa and other sub-Saharan countries for Britain in the recent past. Thousands more have gone to other rich countries.

The fiscal benefits of immigration

A recent study for the British Home Office has calculated the taxes paid by the immigrant population and the amount of government money they receive in the form of welfare payments, health services etc.[13] It estimates that the total taxes paid by immigrants exceed government expenditure on them by £2.6 billion. This is looks a large sum, but in fact it is very small. It is equivalent to 0.3 per cent of GDP, and is less than three months productivity growth. Every decade, the normal process of raising efficiency generates a permanent increase in national income that is 40 times greater than the estimated net fiscal contribution of immigrants to the rest of the society. Moreover, the above figure of £2.6 billion is probably an overestimate, since it ignores the additional public expenditure required to deal with the educational, environmental and social problems arising from large-scale immigration. Britain has undoubtedly gained a great deal in cultural, intellectual and economic terms from certain types of immigration, but the net fiscal transfer of immigrants as a whole to the rest of the population is small. The picture is probably similar in most other rich countries.

Inequality

If all countries in the world were economically developed, then employment and business opportunities would be spread fairly evenly across the globe, and there would be no systematic economic pressures for large-scale migration. In the absence of controls, some individuals would migrate across national boundaries for personal or professional reasons, but such flows would be mostly modest and uncontroversial. This is the present situation within the

European Union. Per capita incomes across the countries of the Union are now similar and the incentive to migrate is quite small. Despite the abolition of migration controls within the Union, the overwhelming majority of citizens prefer to remain in their native country. This situation may change radically following EU enlargement when poorer countries such as Poland, Romania and, eventually, Turkey are admitted to the Union.

There are also natural disasters, wars and civil disturbances to consider. If all countries in the world were prosperous, such events would continue to occur, but they might be less frequent and on average less catastrophic than today. Moreover, much of the migration provoked by such events would be temporary. When refugees arrive in a rich country fleeing a crisis in a poor country, many of them wish to remain when the crisis is over and things return to normal. Life is much better where they are. This is illustrated by the Afghan crisis. According to the UNHCR, one and a half million of the refugees who were housed in camps in Pakistan have now voluntarily returned to Afghanistan. Economic conditions are so bad in Pakistan that they have no incentive to remain. In contrast, few of the Afghans who managed to enter the rich countries want to return home. Many of them might have begun as genuine political or war refugees, but they now have a strong economic incentive to remain in the rich countries.

In a prosperous world, mass migration of a permanent nature would be unusual. However, this is not the world we inhabit today. There are huge international differences in per capita income and economic opportunity, and there is a huge reservoir of people who would migrate to the rich countries if there were no controls. As it is, many evade the controls or manipulate the courts and the regulations for economic advantage.

What is to be done?

Much of the concern in rich countries about immigration comes from the fact that the potential flow of migrants is so great. Present controls are seen as a leaky barrier against a potentially huge inflow of economic migrants. Most Europeans would like to see a more effective control over immigration and many look towards present day Australia for an example. Personally, I am not sure what is the best way to control immigration, although I am convinced of the need for clear immigration rules that are effectively policed. For the reasons given above, I am also opposed to mass immigration into Britain.

There is no need for controls on the movement of citizens within the existing European Union of 15 countries because living standards are similar and there is no economic incentive for mass migration. The same might well be true if barriers between the EU and other rich countries such as Australia or Japan were lowered. However, without barriers against immigration from poor countries, there would be a massive and unacceptable inflow of migrants into the rich countries. For this reason, I see no alternative but support what is known pejoratively as 'Fortress Europe'. I also believe that Britain should retain her existing independent system of immigration controls to reinforce the wider EU system of controls. In addition, immigration from future members of the EU should be restricted until their economies have converged more closely to those of existing members such as Britain.

Retaining the barriers against outsiders is only one aspect of the problem. Britain must also decide how many and what kind of immigrants to admit. We must accept our fair share of genuine asylum seekers, although their admission should normally be on temporary basis until they can safely go home. Permanent residence should only be granted to those who have been legally resident in Britain for some years, or for whom there is no realistic prospect of a safe return to their country of origin within a reasonable time frame. Asylum should not be seen as an automatic passport to permanent residence. We must also find ways to integrate permanent immigrants in a way that preserves the coherence and sense of identity of our nation.

Externally, we must help to reduce the pressures that lead to mass migration. This is a moral and practical imperative. We must become more active in dealing with emergencies that displace large numbers of people from their homelands. This requires action across a wide front. Despite the rhetoric, many rich countries are niggardly in their provision of foreign aid, and they pursue trade and other economic polices that are sometimes very damaging to poor countries. This is not the place to examine what a good development policy should be. I just wish to make the point that it is not morally acceptable just to put up the barriers and say 'Keep Out!' We must also help to tackle the inequalities that drive so many people to leave their homelands and take such risks in pursuit of a better life.

Less inequality would mean less incentive for mass migration, and hence less need for controls to keep out immigrants. The ultimate aim should be to reach the point where all countries enjoy a reasonable standard of living and there is no longer the economic incentive for mass migration. In such a world, most of the existing barriers against migration could be dismantled so that people could move freely from country to country. There would be no mass migration, but just a gradual and beneficial diffusion of people across national frontiers. Because of the incremental nature of the process, national communities would evolve slowly at a pace that did not disrupt their sense of historical continuity.

Notes

David Coleman

1 Tannahill, J.A., *European Voluntary Workers in Britain*, Manchester: Manchester University Press, 1958.

2 Coleman, D.A. and Salt, J., *The British Population: patterns, trends and processes*, Oxford: Oxford University Press, 1992, ch. 11, p. 12.

3 *Immigration and Nationality Department Annual Report 1994*, London: Home Office 1994, p. iii.

4 Office for National Statistics, *International Migration Statistics 2000*, Series MN No. 27, London: The Stationery Office, 2002.

5 *Asylum Statistics United Kingdom 2001*, Home Office Statistical Bulletin 09/02, London: The Home Office, 2002, table 6.1.

6 http://www.migrationwatchuk.org

7 Office for National Statistics, *International Migration. Interim estimates: net flow up to 126,000 in 2001*, 2003. http://www.statistics.gov.uk/cci/nugget.asp?id=260 Office for National Statistics, *Interim Revised Migration Estimates: Explanatory Notes*, http://www.statistics.gov.uk/cci/nugget.asp?vlnk=507

8 Home Office, *Fairer, Faster and Firmer - A Modern Approach to Immigration and Asylum*, Cm 4018, (The White Paper on Immigration and Asylum) London: The Stationery Office, 1998, p. 13.

9 Home Office, *Migration: An Economic and Social Analysis*, Research, Development and Statistics Directorate, Occasional Paper No. 67, London: Home Office, 2001; Gott, C. and Johnston, K., *The Migrant Population in the UK: Fiscal Effects*, Home Office, Research, Development and Statistics Directorate, Occasional Paper No. 77, London: Home Office, 2002.

10 Roche, B., Speech on Migration to Institute of Public Policy Research (IPPR), London: IPPR, 2000.

11 Home Office, *Secure Borders, Safe Haven: Integration with Diversity in Modern Britain*, (White Paper) London, The Stationery Office, 2001, p. 9.

12 Coleman, D.A., Compton. P. and Salt, J., 'The demography of migrant populations: the case of the UK', in Compton, P., Haug, W. and Courbage, Y. (eds), *The Demographic Characteristics of Immigrant Populations*, Population Studies No. 38, Strasburg: Council of Europe, 2002, pp. 497-52.

13 GLA, *Planning for London's Growth: Statistical Basis for the Mayor's Spatial Development Strategy*, London: Greater London Authority, 2002.

14 GAD, *National Population Projections, 2000 based*, Series PP2, No. 23, London: The Stationery Office, 2002.

15 Home Office, *Migration: an economic and social analysis*, Research, Development and Statistics Directorate, Occasional Paper No. 67, London: Home Office, 2001

16 Coleman, D.A., 'Replacement Migration, or Why Everyone is Going to Have to Live in Korea: a fable for our times from the United Nations', *Philosophical Transactions of the Royal Society*, B. 357, 2002, pp. 583-98.

17 http://www.gad.gov/population/2001/methodology/varassumptions.html

18 Compton. P. and Courbage, Y. in Compton *et al*, *The Demography of Migrant Groups in Certain European States*, in press.

19 Murphy, M., 'The Impact of Migration on Population Composition: The British Case', in Voets, S., Schoorl, J. and de Bruijn, B., *The Demographic Consequences of International Migration, NIDI Report No. 44*, The Hague: Netherlands Interdisciplinary Demographic Institute, 1995, pp. 207 - 224.

20 United Nations, *Replacement Migration: Is it a Solution to Declining and Ageing Populations?*, New York: United Nations, 2000.

21 Shaw, C. 'United Kingdom Population Trends in the 21st Century', *Population Trends*(103): 37 - 46, 2001.

22 Dobson, J., Koser, K., McLaughlan, G. and Salt, J., *International Migration and the United Kingdom: Recent patterns and trends*, Home Office Research,

Development and Statistics Directorate, Occasional Paper No 75, London: Home Office, 2001.

23 Office for Standards in Education (OFSTED), Annual Report of HM Chief Inspector of Schools: Standards and Quality in Education 2001/02, London: The Stationery Office, 2003, para. 423. www.official-documents.co.uk/document/deps/ofsted/hc286/286-01.htm

24 Sly, F., Thair, T., *et al.* 'Trends in the Labour Market Participation of Ethnic Groups', *Labour Market Trends*, December 1999: 631 - 639; Salt, J. and Clarke, J., 'Foreign Labour in the United Kingdom: patterns and trends', *Labour Market Trends*, October 2001: 473 - 483.

25 Smith, J.P. and Edmonston, B. (eds), *The New Americans. Economic, Demographic and Fiscal Effects of Immigration*, Washington DC: National Academy Press, 1997.

26 Borjas, G.J., *Heaven's Door: Immigration Policy and the American Economy*, Princeton: Princeton University Press, 1999.

27 Schultz-Nielsen, M.L., *The Integration of Non-Western Immigrants in a Scandinavian Labour Market: the Danish Experience*, Copenhagen: Statistics Denmark, 2001.

28 Jones, K. and Smith, A.D., *The Economic Impact of Commonwealth Immigration*, Cambridge: National Institute for Economic and Social Research, 1970.

29 Gott, and Johnston, *The Migrant Population in the UK: Fiscal Effects*, Home Office, 2002.

30 Oppenheim, C. and Harker, L., *Poverty: The Facts*, London: Child Poverty Action Group, 1996.

31 Smith, D.J., 'Race, Crime and Criminal Justice', in Maguire, M., Morgan, R. and Reiner, R., *The Oxford Handbook of Criminology*, Oxford: Clarendon Press, 1994, pp. 1041-117; Home Office, *Statistics on Race and the Criminal Justice System 2000*, London: Home Office, 2000. http://www.homeoffice.gov.uk/rds/index.htm

32 Dobson, Koser, McLaughlan and Salt, *International Migration and the United Kingdom: Recent patterns and trends*, 2001.

33 OECD, *Trends in International Migration: SOPEMI 2002*, Paris: OECD, 2002, table 1.14.

34 Qualifications and Curriculum Authority, 'Respect for All: reflecting cultural diversity through the national curriculum', 2003. www.qca.org.uk/ca/inclusion/respectforall

35 Berthoud, R., 'Family Formation in Multicultural Britain: three patterns of diversity', Paper 2000/34, Working Papers of the Institute for Social and Economic Research, Colchester, University of Essex, 2000.

36 Immigrant Statistics Unit, 'Population of New Commonwealth and Pakistani Ethnic Origin: new projections', *Population Trends* 16: 22-27, 1979.

37 Haskey, J. (ed.), 'Population projections by ethnic group: a feasibility study', Studies on Medical and Population Subjects No. 67, London: The Stationery Office, 2002.

38 Macperhson, Sir William, *The Stephen Lawrence Inquiry*, Report of an Inquirey by Sir William Macpherson of Cluny, Cm 4262-I, London: The Stationery Office, 1999.

Tamar Jacoby

1 Portes, A. and Rumbaut, R.G., *Children of Immigrants Longitudinal Study,* University of California Press and the Russell Sage Foundation, 2001.

2 Portes and Rumbaut, *Children of Immigrants Longitudinal Study,* 2001.

Robert Rowthorn

1 Much of the information in this section is from the website of MigrationWatchUK.

2 *International Migration 2001 – Interim Estimates,* ONS, Table 1. Note that this figure refers only to non-British citizens. It does not include migration by British citizens. According to the interim estimates

(which exclude asylum seekers' dependants), there was a net loss of 56,300 British citizens through migration in 2001 and a net gain of 182,100 non-British citizens. Combining these flows yields an overall total of 125,700 for net migration. It is this last figure that is normally cited by those wishing to belittle the impact of migration.

3 *Asylum Statistics, United Kingdom 2001,* Office for National Statistics, Table 6.1.

4 The percentages is in this paragraph are from *Population Trends*, Autumn 2001, p. 9, table 1.

5 Data given in the US Census of Population implies that 12.3 per cent of the US population were first generation immigrants in 2001.

6 The exact figure depends on the fertility of the ethnic minority population. Suppose that the natural growth rate of this population is 0.5 per cent per annum and that the net immigration of ethnic minority people is 100 thousand per annum. Given these assumptions, the ethnic minority population rises from 4.0 million in 2000 to 10.8 million (16 per cent of the total population) in 2050. If we assume that the natural growth rate is 1.5 per cent per annum, the size of the ethnic minority population in 2050 is 15.9 million (22 per cent of the total population).

7 The figure of 7.8 per cent refers to 2001-02 and is from the *UK Yearbook 2003* (ONS), p. 94, Table 9.7.

8 These projections are based on tables 2.8.1 and 10.6.1 of the *UK Christian Handbook of Religious Trends*, 2000/2, Christian Research.

9 For a stimulating discussion of this issue see, Parekh, B., *Rethinking Multiculturalism*, Palgrave, 2000.

10 Teitelbaum, M.S. and Winter, J., *A Question of Numbers: high migration, low fertility, and the politics of national identity*, New York: Hill & Wang, 1998, p. 79.

11 Coleman, D., 'Replacement migration, or why everyone is going to have to live in Korea: a fable for our times from the United Nations', *Philosophical Transactions of the Royal Society* B, 2001.

12 *British Medical Journal*, 13 July 2002, p. 66.

13 Gott, C. and Johnston, K., *The Migrant Population in the UK: Fiscal Effects*, RDS Occasional Paper No. 77, London: Home Office, 2002.